MADURA

A TOURIST'S GUIDE

MADURA

A TOURIST'S GUIDE

ILLUSTRATED

GYAN

Published by

Gyan Publishing House
5, Ansari Road
Daryaganj, New Delhi-110002
Phone: 011-47034999, 9811692060
E-mail: books@gyanbooks.com

Distribution Network
gyanbooks.com
India, USA, Canada, UK, Australia, France

ISBN : 978-81-212-3733-8 (PB)
First Published, Madras, 1913

2nd Impression 2020

Printed at: Gyan Press, Delhi.

Madura, A Tourist's Guide

MADURA
A TOURIST'S GUIDE

HIGGINBOTHAM & CO.,
MADRAS.

1913.

Bird's Eye View of Madura Town, Eastern side.

From a Photo by J. W. H. Joshua, Madura

PREFACE.

This little book was undertaken on the casual suggestion of a distinguished European Educationist since retired from the Indian Service. It is hoped that when a stray copy of it falls into his hands in his far-off Irish home it will serve to call forth pleasant memories.

THE AUTHOR.

CONTENTS.

PAGE

INTRODUCTION ... ...

CHAPTER

I.—TOPOGRAPHY, CLIMATE, ETC. ... 12

II.—THE POLITICAL HISTORY OF THE MADURA COUNTRY 15

THE MINAKSHI TEMPLE 64

FESTIVALS 108

THE PERUMAL KOVIL AND OTHER TEMPLES 118

THE TIRUMAL NAIK'S MAHAL AND OTHER BUILDINGS 123

III.—THE MADURA MUNICIPALITY ... 134

IV.—THE PEOPLES OF MADURA 139

V.—OCCUPATIONS, TRADES, ARTS AND INDUSTRIES 169

VI.—EDUCATIONAL AND OTHER INSTITUTIONS 179

VII.—THE HISTORY OF THE JESUIT MISSION IN MADURA 188

LIST OF ILLUSTRATIONS.

PAGE

Bird's eye view of Madura town, eastern side F'piece.
Horse-Court of the Temple, Tiruparakunram, Madura 13
The God and Goddess of the Temple, Madura... 65
South Tower of the Temple, Madura ... 74
Front Entrance to the Shrine of the Temple, Madura 76
The Golden Lily Tank, Western side, inside the Temple 80
The Thousand Pillars Mantapam, a side view... 97
The Thousand Pillars Mantapam, an interior view 100
Western Entrance of the Pudu Mantapam ... 104
A Car Procession... 108
Gods of the Kochadai Iyyanar Temple, Madura. 113
Goddess Kali and God Karupanasamy, Madura. 119
Front Entrance of Tirumal Naik's Palace ... 123
Pillars, Northern side, inside the Palace ... 127
Southern Row of Pillars, The Palace ... 128
View inside the Palace 130
Big Teppa Tank, Western side 132
Big Teppa Tank, another view 133
Palias, or Jungle people, Madura Hills ... 139
A Street View 169

INTRODUCTION.

THE city of Madura, situated on the South Indian Railway, 347 miles south of Madras, is the second largest city in the Madras Presidency. Although it is in a flourishing condition to-day it has suffered many changes of fortune during its long life of two thousand odd years. New dynasties appeared upon its soil from time to time, ruled a few centuries and disappeared successively, but the city has survived and is to-day as prosperous as, if not more than it ever was in its palmiest days in the past. Unlike many other ancient cities which have disappeared or fallen into decay for want of adaptability or of such varied advantages as are required to meet the needs of changing times and circumstances, Madura has enjoyed rare longevity and seems to possess a marvellous capacity to adapt itself to the altered conditions of modern times. And under the strong and peaceful rule of the British it has been growing by leaps and bounds. The forces tending to growth are still in full swing and considering the tendency to urban life evinced by the

Indian people in recent decades the possibilities of its expansion in the near future seem to be boundless. The town has already outstripped its natural topographical limits and is extending on all sides. Some time ago the plague was almost at its gate threatening an unexpected calamity, but thanks to the unflinching efforts of a dutiful district ruler, the epidemic was successfully warded off and the town saved from its dire ravages.

During the third and second centuries before Christ, when the maritime trade of the ancient Dravidians was fast leaving their hands owing to causes far beyond their control, and the activities of the people were diverted from the sea to the land as a result of the rise of the young kingdoms of Chera and Chola, the Pandyans felt the need for a capital farther inland and Madura offered perhaps the best inducement, being situated in the centre of the Vaigai Valley—in the midst of a large plain, backed up in the west by the Western Ghats, bounded on the east by the sea and separated on the north from the kingdom of the warlike Cholas by a series of low hills, the offshoots of the Western Ghats, and the thick forests enveloping them. (The remnants of these even after centuries of reckless denudation are known at present as the Ayyalur forests). The new capital was sufficiently far from the reach of the Singhalese foes on the maritime side where the Pandyans were rapidly losing their advantage and it brought them nearer their land enemies with whom all their struggle lay in the future. What was more, the place carried with it divine sanction, having been christened by Siva himself. This condescension of the Lord of the Kadamba forest afforded a peculiar satisfaction to the religious sentiments of the primitive people. The city soon became the busy capital of the most powerful and wealthy kingdom in the south and the centre of early Dravidian culture and civilization. As the seat of the Tamil Academy it attracted to itself all the learning of the age and even in the succeeding centuries when the power of the Pandyans was not at its highest, when they had to render tribute to the new dynasty of Pallavas ruling from the north, and when there were other cities equally large and famous, Madura still continued to be a place of pilgrimage and the one seat of learning in the south. We read in the lives of the

Tamil poets and saints of the third and fourth centuries how they would not rest satisfied until their literary productions received the *imprimatur* of the Madura Tamil Sangham. Tiruvalluvar and Auvai treaded their weary way to Madura to receive the hall-mark of the Academy. According to the Puranic history of the locality, it would appear that it was also the scene of a triangular contest between Buddhism, Jainism, and Saivism. Later in the days when the Pallavas and the Cholas established their supremacy over the south, the city suffered partial decadence with its rulers, until at the commencement of the 13th century it revived with the revival of the Pandyan power under Sundara Pandya (circa 1290 A. D.) and soon regained its lost prosperity. Marco Polo, who touched the Coromandel Coast about this time, heard of the enormous wealth of the Pandyan king derived from a lucrative pearl trade. Then followed a period of darkness. When the curtain rises again in the middle of the 16th century, we find that the city has undergone complete transformation under the wise and energetic rule of Visvanatha, the first and perhaps the greatest of the Naik kings of Madura. Round about the small ancient shrine, new walls and towers have risen. The deity has been housed in a new and grand temple. The old make-believe fort walis of mud and palisade have disappeared, and in their place, streets are arranged in symmetrical order in concentric squares, the whole town being enclosed in a strong stone fort of 72 bastions, each with its proper guard. Here are the beginnings of the modern city of Madura. The main features indicated above survive to the present day. A century later, in the days of Tirumala, it attained to the zenith of its prosperity and possessed all the traditional marks of the magnificent capital of an eastern potentate rolling in wealth and luxury—royal palaces, mansions of nobles, pavilions, temples, choultries, barracks, pleasure gardens, and tanks.

The writer of the Madura District Gazetteer, following the learned author of the "Madura Country" has questioned the claims of Madura to the enviable position of the capital of the Naik kingdom. Both authors have dwelt at some length on the comparative merits of Madura and Trichinopoly and have pointed out that Trichinopoly, with its almost impregnable rock fort, its never-failing Cauvery, and its healthy climate, was by nature far superior to Madura, where the fort was on level ground, the Vaigai was usually dry, and fever was almost endemic. They seem to deplore the lack of wisdom exhibited by the earlier Naik kings in preferring Madura to Trichinopoly for their capital and to applaud the action of the later kings of the dynasty in moving their court to the latter city. They omit to explain how then in spite of such disadvantages Madura persisted as the capital, not only of the Naiks, but of the earlier and later dynasties that ruled in the Madura country, and have failed to look for any special natural advantages possessed by the town which must have outweighed those considerations of defence, water-supply, and sanitation, in respect of which points, Madura was, and is inferior to Trichinopoly. But these are not the only nor the chief points for consideration in the choice of a capital. The deficient water-supply of Madura was made up for by the construction of tanks in the city. As a fact Madura was not more subject to the ravages of fever than Trichinopoly, where during the floods in the river fever was quite common. The question really resolves itself into this, given the boundaries of the Naik kingdom and the nature of the neighbourhood, which of these two places was the better fitted to be the seat of the Government? It has already been pointed out how Madura occupies a central position in the midst of a plain with well defined natural boundaries. The Madura country forms a distinct geographical unit—a natural region. Now it is a well-known principle of history that capitals of States tend to gravitate towards the natural centre of their territories. In the light of this principle it becomes easy to understand how Madura, the natural centre of a geographical region, became also the political capital of a kingdom whose boundaries coincided more or less with those of the natural region. From this point of view, Trichinopoly, situated on the borders of the kingdom, was least fitted to be the capital. As a frontier garrison with its impregnable rock fort commanding the chief routes, its pre-eminence was inestimable. But being on the borders of the Naik kingdom it was, as the following pages on history will show, open to frequent attacks from the neighbouring enemies. Madura was situated farther into the interior, well sheltered from attack by a large belt of surrounding country and several strong frontier fortresses. Trichinopoly itself was such a fortress and the chief gate of the kingdom. Two more fortresses lay on the routes to Madura—Dindigul and Natham. A reference to the local history shows us that several times Dindigul bore the brunt of the attacks from the armies of Mysore, and on each occasion repulsed the enemy with disastrous results. Thus Madura lay beyond the easy reach of the neighbouring enemies. Before they could strike at her, they had to subjugate the strong fortresses of Trichinopoly or Dindigul and thus allow Madura sufficient time to get ready. Such retired safety could not be thought of in the case of Trichinopoly. The fate of Vijayanagar must be a standing object-lesson to those that would found their capital on the naturally insecure borders of the kingdom. When danger threatened, the Naik kings temporarily camped at Trichinopoly, but they always retired to Madura which they made the seat of government, culture, and civilization. The removal of the Court to Trichinopoly in later times paved the way for the easy and sudden overthrow of the dynasty by the Mahomedans.

The city whose foundations were laid under the watchful and paternal care of Visvanatha and which it was the ambition of Tirumala to make so grand and glorious as to be a reflection of Vijayanagar in the south, was suddenly shaken and its beautiful edifices pulled down by the vandalistic schemes of a hare-brained successor of Tirumala, who conceived the ingenious idea of removing the edifices to Trichinopoly. This did more for the disfigurement of the town than even the later British conquest. When the city passed into the hands of the East India Company, the fortifications were pulled down, the stones from the fort walls were used for more utilitarian purposes; to build a causeway across the Vaigai, and to fill up the ditch that surrounded the fort. With the recent introduction of the system of water-supply by underground pipes several of the old tanks have been levelled up with mud and sand and turned into market places, flower gardens, and recreation grounds.

The Future of Madura.

The natural causes that favoured her choice as the capital of the Pandyan and Naik kings in ancient and mediæval times still operate to give her the leading place among south Indian mofussil towns. The political importance of her central situation has dwindled into insignificance on the merging of this part of the country into the larger political organization of the British Presidency. Still she is the centre to which all the trade of the district converges. The location at Madura of the new Ramnad district offices also has added to her administrative importance and attracted a large office-going population from the surrounding country. The impetus from this source, however, can only be of a temporary nature. The future of Madura seems to lie in her industries. With a large cotton-growing district in the neighbourhood, with one or two spinning mills and a vigorous industrial population whose hereditary profession is weaving and who manifest great powers of organization for industrial purposes, the future possibilities of the local weaving industry are immense. When the hope entertained for electric power from Periyar is realised, the industry will receive an additional impetus. Cheap power will facilitate the introduction of machinery to a larger extent and it will not be too much to prophesy that Madura will become the Manchester of Southern India. The opening of a harbour at Mantapam and the completion of the railway to Ceylon will considerably enhance her importance as a railway junction and afford further facilities for direct foreign trade.

CHAPTER I.

TOPOGRAPHY, CLIMATE, ETC.

MADURA is situated on the bank of the river Vaigai at an elevation of 330 feet above the sea level. It may be said to consist roughly of 5 parts—a central part and extensions on four sides: (1) The central part consists of the temple square and the streets running parallel to the walls of the temple in squares—the outermost square being identical with the old fort walls. This part is very thickly congested, being occupied on one side mostly by Brahmins. (2) The extension to the east is along the road leading to the grand Vandiyur tank. The road is lined on both sides with the bungalows of the European residents of the town. One of them, known as the Teppakulam Bungalow, contains a costly cabinet of carved wood and ivory of the finest workmanship and with an interesting history of its own. (3) The southern extension is a disorderly heap of houses and cottages belonging to weavers and other lower classes. (4) In the west beyond the railway line a fine colony has been built for railway servants. On the way to the colony stands the

Horse-Court of the Temple, Tiruparaknuram, Madura.

From a Photo by J. W. H. Joshua, **Madura.**

new Travellers' Bungalow and farther west on the other side of the colony is the District Jail. (5) It is in the north, on the northern bank of the river, that the greatest extension on modern lines of town construction is expected to take place. Already some important buildings, such as the Tamkam Pavilion, the American College and Hostel, the English and Union Clubs are situated there. The new office buildings, and residential quarters for officers are in the course of construction and sites are being rapidly bought up for houses for the office-going native population. There is yet unlimited space available for recreation grounds, parks, gardens, walks, and so forth. Farther north, on the road is a wide and splendid race-ground. In the tanks beyond, which are really small lakes, snipe abound and Europeans frequent them for snipe shooting.

The river is crossed by a bridge and a causeway. The view from the bridge of the river and its banks thickly studded with cocoanut palms and domes and towers is a very picturesque one. The river is dry during the greater part of the year. But there is always an under current which is easily reached by digging a foot or two in the river-bed. Such diggings are called "Odugāls" and form a perennial source of water-supply.

Madura is anything but a sanitarium. The summer heat during the months of April, May and June is terrible. In July the south-westerlies commence and moderate the heat. The only other season known is the winter, which is not cold enough to be recuperative. In old times at particular seasons, winds from the Alagar Kovil forests used to cause epidemics of fever in the town. The forests have largely been denuded, but fever, cholera, small-pox and other diseases continue to be unfailing visitors at the changes of the seasons. Rain falls mostly in winter, but some usually falls in July. The average rainfall during the year is 35·00 inches. The sites and places worth visiting in Madura are many. Detailed descriptions of most of them will be found in the following pages.

CHAPTER II.

HISTORY.

The history of the city of Madura is bound up with the history of Southern India and it is marked off naturally into three periods—the ancient, the mediæval and the modern.

The Ancient Period.—The ancient period may be said to begin as early as the times of Megasthenes, the Greek ambassador in the court of Chandragupta Maurya, about 320 B. C. The kingdom of Pandya and its capital Madura are mentioned by the classical geographers Pliny (*cir.* 77 A. D.) and Ptolemy (140 A. D.), and the discovery of Roman coins of the time of Augustus in the vicinity of Madura has led to the belief that a Roman Colony existed there in those times in pursuit of eastern commerce. References to the Pandya kingdom are also found in Asoka's inscriptions.

Origin of the Pandyas.

From the earliest historical times the extreme south of India comprising the districts of Madura and Tinnevelly was ruled by the Pandyans. Tradition ascribes the origin of the dynasty to one of three brothers who lived at Korkai at the mouth of the Tambraparani river in the Tinnevelly district. Of the three brothers Chola and Chera went forth from their country to conquer new lands while Pandya remained at home and became the ancestor of the Pandyas.

Derivation of the name Madura.

According to the Sthala Purana, the Local Chronicle, which records the doings of the early Pandyas, Sundaresvara the local deity appeared one day before the then ruling king Kulasekhara Pandya in a dream and commanded him to build a city round a shrine in the middle of the adjoining Kadamba forest near his capital Kalyanapura. The divine order was instantly obeyed and when the king knew not what name to give to the new city, the deity again appeared before him dancing and sanctified the new city with a shower of nectar from his hoary locks of hair. And this incident suggested the name of the city, Madura, which means sweetness. Another derivation is given by modern scholars who believe that an Aryan colony settled in the place and the colonists called it after their famous city of Madhura, the modern Muttra on the banks of the Jumna.

Ancient History.

Except for what is preserved in the Local Chronicle referred to above the early history of the Pandyas is lost in obscurity and it is only here and there enlightened by contemporary native literature or the accounts of foreign travellers or by stone inscriptions. According to the late Mr. Kanakasabhai Pillay, the author of "The Tamils Eighteen Hundred Years Ago" the earliest historical personality of any fame is Ugraperuvaludi (128-140 A. D.) and his name is memorable as the king at whose court the famous Tiruvalluvar the author of the sacred didactic poem—the Kural—and his talented sister Auvaiyar, flourished amidst a brilliant galaxy of 48 poets. Of the later kings it will perhaps be sufficient to mention Nedumaran for it was at his court that Tirugnana Sambandhar, the great saivite saint, flourished. He is credited to have miraculously cured the king of a fever which his Jain gurus were not able to cure and thus converted the king from Jainism to Saivitism.

To the close of the 9th century A. D., the Pandyans seem to have been supreme in the south and some time during that period to have ruled over the Cholas. There are inscriptions recording many wars between the Pandyas, the Pallavas and the Chalukyas. The Pandyans seem to have been feudatories paying tribute to the Pallavas but permitted to rule over their own country. In the tenth century A. D., the Cholas rose into power and in their turn conquered the Pandyas. Parantaka I (906-946 A. D.) and Raja Raja (985-1017) are great names in the history of the Cholas as conquerors of the Pandya kingdom. During the reign of Rajadhiraja Chola (1018-1053) the Pandyans rebelled but were sternly suppressed. The Cholas now supreme in tho south styled themselvs Chola Pandyas. Their supremacy lasted till the middle of the 12th century when a great effort was successfully made by the Pandyas to throw off the yoke of the Cholas. At the close of the century a great Singhalese invasion of the Madura country took place and the Pandyas were defeated thrice successively. From the beginning of the 13th century the

The Cholas at Madura.

The Chola Pandyas.

Pandyan history becomes continuous and is copiously illuminated by inscriptions. Māravarman Sundara Pandya (1216-1236) is said to have captured the Chola capital but most graciously restored it to the owner. One of his descendants Jatāvarman Sundara Pandya I (1251-1261) invaded Ceylon and carried off a great booty and extended his dominions on all sides, defeating even the Hoysalas of Mysore in a great battle. Māravarman Kulasekhara (1268-1308) was a famous king in his days and is mentioned by the Mahomedan historians of India. His successor, more probably perhaps his joint ruler, Jatāvarman Sundara Pandya II is identical with the Sender Bandi of the famous Italian traveller Marco Polo.

The Pandyas again supreme.

In the beginning of the 14th century happened the first invasion of Southern India by the Mahomedans under Malik Kafur, the General of Allauddin Khalji, Emperor of Delhi. He swept across the country as far as Ramesvaram, sacking Madura on the way. Nelson in his 'Madura Country' quotes some native manuscripts in support of this invasion and the establishment

Mahomedan Invasions.

of a Mahomedan dynasty at Madura which is said to have ruled for a period of 48 years. The Mahomedan authority was overthrown and ousted out of Madura about the year 1365 by Kampanna Udayar, a General of the Vijayanagar Empire. His descendants ruled at Madura till 1404 as feudatories of the Vijayanagar Emperor. After that date the administration was entrusted into the hands of a number of chieftains bearing Telugu names and titles until the establishment of the Naik dynasty in 1559. During this period of Vijayanagar domination only the foreign affairs were conducted by the imperial authority. The imperial army watched the safety of the Pandyan kingdom from foreign aggression. The internal administration of the country was still in the hands of the Pandyas.

Vijayanagar intervenes.

The Mediaeval Period.—The year 1559 marks the beginning of an important epoch in the history of Madura. In that year Virasekhara Chola, the King of Tanjore, invaded the Pandyan kingdom, captured the city and annexed it to his dominions. The Pandya

The establishment of the Naik dynasty.

and his young prince fled and once again sought the protection and support of the Vijayanagar Emperor. Enraged at the effrontery of a vassal, the Emperor despatched his Commander-in-Chief Nagama Naik against the rebellious chief of Tanjore. The campaign was quite an easy one and the mission was performed without even a show of resistance. Nagama Naik marched into the town and occupied it. But strange to say instead of carrying out the imperial orders he set aside the Pandyan king and made himself the ruler of the country. When the news of the defection of one of the chief and trusted generals reached the ears of the Emperor he was filled with disappointment, rage and revenge.

A Romance.

Hastily he summoned a council of state. After explaining to them the facts of the case, the Emperor demanded in an angry and passionate tone "Is there none among you so brave that shall bring me this traitor's head?" There was no reply; the councillors sat mute looking at one another, each hoping that some one besides himself would stand up to answer. Indeed the query was one that required consideration before replying. Nagama Naik was no mean general; to undertake a campaign against him was to incur a very serious responsibility. Born in poor circumstances, Nagama Naik had been introduced into royal notice and favour and had been appointed store-keeper of the royal mansion. From that peaceful office he turned to the army; by dint of ability, alertness and fidelity he rose from post to post in the state service until he was appointed the Commander-in-Chief of the Southern forces of the Empire, an office of the highest order and of the greatest trust and respectability. He had fought and won laurels in the campaigns against the kings of Bijapur and Golconda. To march against such a veteran, indeed anyone might hesitate. The Emperor repeated the question with greater vehemence and passion. Another pause ensued. Suddenly, from the assembly there stood up a young man on whose face one could read at the same time the play of shame and revenge; it was Visvanatha, the son of the rebellious Nagama Naik. "My lord", said he "I will bring him dead or alive, though he be my own father." The king could not believe his own eyes but the young captain—for he was already in the Imperial army and a favourite with the

Emperor—having assured the Emperor on word of honor of his fidelity and requesting to be sent, Visvanatha Naik set out on the march towards Madura. He met his father in a pitched battle, took him prisoner and sent him in safe custody to his sovereign. He reached Madura, placed the feeble Pandya on the throne and returned to the capital. The Emperor welcomed him with due honor and at the request of the valiant young hero, granted liberty to his father and conferred the governorship of the Pandya kingdom on Visvanatha Naik.

Visvanatha made Governor of the Pandya kingdom.

The incident derives its significance not so much from its romantic nature as from the consequences that flowed therefrom. It turned the whole course of Madura history into a new channel and inaugurated a silent revolution in the politics of Southern India. A wise and efficient rule was substituted in place of the old effete monarchy. The Pandyans, no doubt, continued to rule but only in name. Coins were still struck with the emblem of the fish and grants were made in their name. But the real power had passed irrevocably into the hands of the more powerful governors. The farce of a Supreme Pandya was kept up till the time of Tirumala Naik who threw down the mask and openly declared himself the real and sole sovereign. Hence we may say that the Naik dynasty to which Madura owes so much was founded by Visvanatha and for the next 200 years the annals of Madura are closely bound up with the fortunes of the Naik dynasty.

Early life and character of Visvanatha.

Visvanatha was the first and greatest of the Naik rulers. About the early life of this great man we would fain know but it is involved in the same mystery that surrounds the early days of all great men. Barring legends and traditions that have gathered round his name, we may say that he was the only child of Nagama Naik, born after severe penance. As such we may infer that his early life ought to have received the greatest attention from his father and nowhere in those days could a young man seek for better learning than at Vijayanagar, for under the magnanimous patronage of the court all the learning of the age had centred there and every Emperor was himself a poet and author of real merit. He seems to have been early introduced to the favour of the Rāya and been appointed to various posts in the army which he filled with distinction before he was sent on the expedition against his father.

His work at Madura.

The task that now awaited Visvanatha as Governor of Madura was one of immense difficulty. It was nothing less than the creation of order out of chaos. Two centuries of anarchy, misrule, foreign invasions and internal dissensions had reduced the people to the greatest poverty. The roads had become infested with robbers who carried on their trade in broad daylight. The neighbouring tribes, ever turbulent, had been left to themselves and were not to be easily subdued. The miseries of the people cried aloud for a strong hand to keep the peace and render justice to the weak and the strong. Thus the circumstances called for a firm hand and wise statesmanship. Visvanatha rose equal to the responsibilities of the post. His attention was first of all drawn to the miserable state of the defences of the city. He pulled down the old ramparts and ditch that surrounded the pagoda, laid out a new plan for the city, built agraharams and streets for Brahmins round the temple in squares and constructed an extensive double walled fortress round the city with 72 bastions. This was the beginning of the modern city of Madura and to this day the city has the same set plan. He cleared the jungles that had grown up in the neighbourhood and broke up the gangs of marauders that had made the jungles their stronghold. Having secured the defences of the city, he turned to its water supply and constructed two dams (the Peranai and Chittanai) across the upper courses of the Vaigai and turned off the waters to irrigate the lands round the capital. In a very short time the results of this beneficent policy became apparent. The waning prosperity returned with wonderful rapidity and with it the population multiplied and once more the city was restored to the prosperity and splendour that it had enjoyed in the early days of the Pandyans.

His foreign conquests.

Visvanatha next turned to the extension and consolidation of his dominions. The old Pandyan kingdom had included the districts of Trichinopoly, Madura, and Tinnevelly. During the recent troubles parts had become independent and had defied all authority. Trichinopoly had fallen into the hands of the Cholas of Tanjore. It was situated at the northern entrance of the kingdom and commanded the grand trunk road from the north to Ramesvaram. Until it was occupied, the safety of the kingdom could not be ensured. So Visvanatha negotiated for an exchange of the fortress of Vallam near Tanjore for Trichinopoly. Partly by persuasion and partly by threats from the Raya, the Chola was induced to cede the much-coveted place which was immediately fortified and strengthened. The relics of the old fort can still be traced more easily at Trichinopoly than those at Madura. The temple of Srirangam was repaired and endowed with funds. The roads were made clear of wild beasts and highway robbers and once more the train of pilgrims from the north wended their way to Ramesvaram unmolested, and the town of Trichinopoly was on the fair way to prosperity.

Next he turned to the affairs in the south. Some illegitimate children of the late Pandya had fled to Tinnevelly and there gathered a number of followers and had defied the Naik armies under Arya Naik, the able general and minister, of whom more will be said hereafter.

His southern campaign.

Visvanatha himself came down in person. The campaign proved an arduous one. The five Pandyas declined to come to close quarters and kept up a harassing guerilla warfare. There appeared to be no prospect of a speedy end of the campaign. Bold, audacious and even reckless at times, Visvanatha was a born general and in the present difficulty his resourcefulness did not forsake him. Relying on the strength of his arm and his skill at fencing, he boldly challenged the rebel princes to fight him in single combat five against one, on the condition they should leave the country undisturbed if they were unsuccessful. Be it said to the credit of the opponents that they had the gallantry to fight him one by one. But they were severally defeated and thus was terminated what threatened to be a serious check to the rising power of the Naiks. The moral effects of a defeat would have been disastrous to them. In accordance with his usual policy Visvanatha proceeded to secure the defences of the country and of the town of Tinnevelly; familiarised the people with the blessings of good government and conciliated the Brahmins by building new pagodas, repairing old ones, cutting water courses and policing the highways.

From the south Visvanatha was called away to enforce obedience on a recalcitrant chieftain of Cumbum up the Vaigai valley. The rebel was made to feel the strong hand of Visvanatha and brought back to his senses. The expedition did good to the people, inasmuch as it attracted the attention of the ruler to a neglected but exceedingly fertile corner of the kingdom. This was the last of the military labours of the able Naik.

Extent of Visvanatha's kingdom.

The Kingdom thus united and strengthened covered the modern districts of Trichinopoly, Madura, Tinnevelly and the southern part of Travancore.

Visvanatha's statesmanship.

Great as he was in war, greater still was Visvanatha in the arts of peace. We have spoken of his beneficent measures for the protection of his people. With the far-sighted vision of a statesman he understood the need of an administrative machinery that would work independently of the prince on the throne. The plan that he devised was quite original and well fitted to the circumstances and satisfied the diverse interests of the State. A large number of adherents had followed him all the way from the Telugu country in the hope of winning glory and reward. Their demands had to be satisfied in the first place. Then there were the Tamil hereditary chieftains of the land that naturally viewed with hostility the settlement of the foreign Telugus and had to be conciliated and made to support the new dynasty. Then again the followers of the Pandyans had to be satisfied. Visvanatha parcelled out the conquered lands into a number of feudal domains each under the charge of a feudal lord whose duty it was to maintain a band of retainers in readiness to keep guard over each of the 72 bastions. Thus was created the system of the Poligars that is universal in Southern India.

The Poligar system.

In this policy of conciliation, Visvanatha was ably seconded by his Commander-in-Chief and minister Ariyanayaka Mudali,* whose name we have already mentioned. In fact the Poligar system may be said to owe its inception to the sagacity of this astute minister. There are as many stories current about this great man as about Visvanatha. At this distance of time it is impossible to do justice to the greatness of Ariyanayaka which suffers in comparison by the side of his equally great sovereign Visvanatha. The hall of 1,000 pillars in the Minakshi temple was constructed at his instance and one can see the equestrian statue of this remarkable man at the entrance to the hall. He is said to have been born at Kanchipura, of poor parents of the Vellala caste. There is the stock story told of him also that his greatness was prophesied by a cobra that sheltered him from the heat of the sun by its outspread hood. He seems to have been very quick at figures and became at an early age attached to Nagama Naik on whose death he ably served his son as Dalavai or General. Of his later life we will treat as we proceed.

Visvanatha's minister Ariyanayakam.

---

* *Note.*—This name is variously spelt, Arya Natha, Arya Naik, etc., by different authorities.

After reigning in peace for some time longer, the Maharaja Manya Rajasri Visvanatha Nayana Ayyagaru died in great honor and glory. He was the greatest of his line, a rare soldier and statesman, one who kept the welfare of the public at heart and always worked towards that end.

Death of Visvanatha 1563.

Visvanatha Naik was succeeded by his son Kumara Krishnappa Naik who was also a brave and politic ruler and inherited in a large measure his father's practical sagacity. His reign was marked by the rebellion of Dumbichi Naik and the conquest of the northern part of Ceylon.

His successor Kumara Krishnappa, 1563—1573.

In the second year of his reign, events were happening in the Dekhan that shook the Empire to its very foundations. The Mahomedan Princes against whom the Empire had so long been contending severally, now combined for a united action against the common enemy and marched against Vijayanagar. To withstand this great danger, the Raya had to strain every nerve and so Ariyanayaka was called away from the scene of his labours for the protection of the capital of the Empire. His immediate return from the north seemed impossible. Seizing this favourable opportunity of the absence of the leading man and mistaking the character of the young prince on the throne, Dumbichi Naik, one of the 72 poligars, plotted with a few others and organised a formidable rebellion. The Governor was unprepared for an event of this nature. Allowed to win a success or two, the insurrection grew in a short time into very large proportions—towns and villages were looted and a considerable extent of territory was overrun and Dumbichi Naik entrenched himself behind a strongly fortified camp near Paramakudi to the east of Madura. When the real nature of the trouble was made known, Krishnappa Naik immediately made the necessary arrangements for the protection of his own person and the capital and for the suppression of the rebellion and despatched a force under his general, who was however defeated and killed. In a second engagement, the Madura forces were victorious. The rebel army was defeated, completely routed and dispersed. The rebel

The Rebellion of Dumbichi.

leader was caught. His head was chopped off and sent to the capital and hung up at the gate as a lesson to others of his stamp. The rebellion merely served to test the fitness and determined the survival of the new dynasty. Krishnappa's throne became all the more secure. Though the feud was confiscated, still the generosity of the prince was such that the wife and young children were duly provided for by the grant of a few villages.

The campaign against Ceylon.

During the campaign, Dumbichi had been assisted with men and money by the Rajah of Kandy in Ceylon and Krishnappa determined to teach him a lesson. He put himself at the head of a large army officered by no less than 52 poligars, and marched against the king of Kandy. The army embarked with great pomp and display at Ramesvaram, crossed the narrow channel in native boats and landed safely in Ceylon. An ultimatum was forthwith sent to the ruler of Kandy who was quite unprepared to meet such a foe. Hastily mustering together an army of 14,000, commanded by four of his ministers, he offered battle at a place called Pattalam. In the engagement that followed, by rapid manœuvres and better discipline and the timely arrival of a battalion that had been kept in reserve, the Madura army was completely victorious. Two of the Kandy ministers and five of the generals and a large number of the enemy were taken prisoners and be it said in fairness to the general that all the prisoners were treated with great humanity; their wounds were dressed and medicines and separate tents were provided for the reception of the sick and the wounded. But the enemy had not been crippled. The king was still safe at Kandy. The captured ministers offered to negotiate a peace but to no purpose. So Krishnappa Naik pushed on towards the capital and met another army vastly superior in strength. Just in front of the walls of the city a sanguinary battle was fought. Mere numerical strength could not avail before the better discipline and generalship of the Naik army. The Ceylonese army was defeated and driven out of the field. Though every attempt was made to secure the person of the king alive, he was shot dead by an arrow and when the sun set that day Kandy was at the mercy of the conqueror. Krishnappa occupied the city for three days during which the funeral ceremonies of the dead king were performed with royal honor and his widow and children were liberally provided for. A close relative of Krishnappa was appointed viceroy of the conquered kingdom and Krishnappa returned to Madura. The prompt suppression of Dumbichi's rebellion and the conquest of the north of Ceylon had such a moral effect on the poligars that never again was there any trouble to the close of the reign.

The Naik kingdom of Kandy.

Meanwhile in 1565, the great battle of Talikota had been fought and the Vijayanagar armies defeated in the Dekhan. The enemies marched on the capital and captured it, and began a work of destruction such as has rarely been recorded in history. The fort walls were razed to the ground. Neither palace, temple nor works of art were spared. The whole city was ruthlessly destroyed so that not a vestige remained behind but the shapeless heaps of brick and mortar and a few mutilated works of art that may even to-day be seen as one walks down the extensive ruins of Hampe.

Talikota and its results.

The royal family escaped and set up a new capital at Chandragiri and continued to rule from their new capital. Their suzerainty was in no way destroyed though their prestige was greatly diminished. Annual tributes were still sent to Chandragiri. Ariyanayaka was appointed Commander-in-chief and Minister of the principalities of Mysore, Madura and Tanjore After some time he returned to Madura and settled his family at Sholavandan where his descendants even to this day indulge in the memories of a glorious past.

It is said that the latter days of Krishnappa Naik were spent in founding cities, building agraharams and temples, cutting water courses and many another work of usefulness to the people. After a decade of peaceful and prosperous rule, Krishnappa died in 1573, to the intense grief of the whole people. He was succeeded by his two sons, during whose reign there is nothing very important that will interest the general reader and the kingdom seems to have enjoyed rest under the able administration of Ariyanayaka. The joint rule came to an end in 1595 and the sons of the younger prince succeeded the throne. In

1600 A. D. Ariyanayaka died of ripe old age. He is one of the greatest figures that we come across in the history of Southern India. He had been the right-hand man of Visvanatha on the founding of the Nayak dynasty, the sole guide of Krishnappa and his sons. It was equally due to his fostering care that the young and rickety kingdom was enabled to tide over its early struggles. His name was held in awe and respect throughout Mysore, Tanjore and Madura. The poligar system owed its inception to the genius of Ariyanayaka Mudali.

The joint rule also seems to have come to an end shortly after; for Visvappa died in 1601 and Lingayya in 1602. They were succeeded by Lingayya's son, Muthukrishnappa. But an uncle of this prince, one Kasturi Rangayya, being an ambitious man, usurped the throne and the adherents of the young prince rose against the usurper, whom they murdered.

Muthu Krishnappa 1602-09.

The only important event of his reign was the restoration of the chief of the Sethupathis whose grandfather had been deprived of his ancestral feud of Ramnad by an early Pandyan. The restored Sethupathi proved himself such a capable administrator that he brought peace and prosperity to the country and once more the grand trunk road to Ramesvaram swarmed with pilgrims. In recognition of his services, he was subsequentl rais.d to the leadership of the 72 poligars. The rema.n ng peaceful days of the reign were employed in the useful work of cutting canals, building temples and agraharams, and laying the foundations f the town of Krishnapura between Madura and Tirupurangundram, the ruins of which may still be traced. He died in 1609, leaving behind three sons, Muthu Virappa, Tirumala, and Kumaramuthu.

Muthu Virappa 1609-23.

Muthu Virappa, the eldest son of the late Naik, reigned till 1622. During his reign there was a Mahomedan invasion from the north which was successfully repulsed. The Mysoreans attacked and invested the fort of Dindigul. The poligar in charge of the fortress won grea fame by driving off the Mysoreans. Besides these minor disturbances we do not know anything about the reign until we come to the memorable rule of Tirumala.

Tirumala Naik 1623-1659.

Tirumala, the brother of the late Naik, succeeded to the throne and ruled for 36 years between 1623 and 1659. He was a great builder and his buildings remain in Madura to the present day. Some of them are described in the following pages. By some he has been considered to be "the greatest without exception of all the rulers of Madura in modern times" (Nelson's "Madura Country"). In our opinion the reign of Tirumala was anything but an unmixed blessing to the Madura country. His fame has been out of all proportion to his deserts and rests mainly on the slender foundation of the few architectural monuments surviving in Madura. Far from being the greatest of the line it appears to us that he can compare favorably neither with Visvanatha Naik, the founder of the Naik dynasty, nor with Mangammal, the talented and high souled Queen Regent; nor even with Kumara Krishnappa, the conqueror of Kandy in Ceylon. Succeeding to the heritage of a great and powerful kingdom, established with very great efforts by Visvanatha Naik and organised with admirable administrative skill by his astute minister Ariya Naik, and in possession of a well filled treasury, resulting from a policy of peaceful reform and retrenchment for over two generations, Tirumala squandered the immense treasures in foreign wars that brought neither territory nor glory and in buildings fitted more for personal enjoyment than for public benefit, and sowed those seeds of hatred in the hearts of the neighbouring princes that brought down foreign nations during the reign of his unfortunate successor, Chokkanatha, and ultimately paved the way for the decay and downfall of the Naik kingdom. From beginning to end his policy in matters of State was ill-advised, ignominious, and singularly lacking in foresight. In the choice of men he showed the greatest incapacity. The services of able men of the type of Ramappaiya and Dalavai Sethupathi were wasted in the hands of a suspicious and intriguing superior.

We hall summarise the events of this so-called "glorious reign" extending over a period of 36 years. Tirumala inaugurated the commencement of his rule in 1623 by declaring himself independent of the Vijayanagar Emperor and made the defensive arrangements necessary to meet the consequences of such a step. That Tirumala was left unpunished immediately for this act of insubordination was due to the fact that the Penukonda branch of the Vijayanagar dynasty had just then come to an end and the other branch had not yet felt itself strong in its new capital at Chandragiri. It was still too much engaged in a life and death struggle with the Mahomedan princes of the Dekhan to pay heed to the events happening in the south.

The first of the series of wars that occupied most of Tirumala's time was waged against Mysore. At the instance of Chama Raja Wodeiyar, Raja of Mysore, a large army under the command of Harasura Nandiraj poured down the ghauts by the Gazulhatty pass near Sathiamangalam, occupied a large extent of the Madura country, marched southwards and attempted to take the strong fortress of Dindigul by storm. The exact cause of the invasion is unknown. Possibly it was undertaken, as Nelson says, in order to avenge the defeat of a Mysore army by one from Madura in a previous reign. More probably, perhaps, it was inspired by orders from the Vijayanagar Emperor to punish the recalcitrant Madura Naik. When the news of the invasion reached the ears of Tirumala, he hastily mustered his forces and despatched them under his able general Ramappaiya, who rallied round him the panic stricken poligars of Dindigul and turned the tables on the enemy by carrying the war into Mysore. There he laid siege to the capital. But in the very hour of victory he had peremptory orders from Tirumala, who had allowed his ears to be poisoned by a court faction against the minister. Like Nelson in the famous battle of the Baltic, the resourceful Dalavay rose equal to the occasion, pretended ignorance of the order until the enemy surrendered and then hastened to the capital with such a formidable force and surrounded by a body of faithful poligars that Tirumala thought it wise to change his attitude immediately and welcome the victorious general with honours and rewards. The Mysore war was thus abandoned when a profitable peace might have been concluded; the loyalty f an able general was tampered with while his services were still required by the State.

A few years after, an event occurred which throws into relief the character of Tirumala Naik. Sadek Tevan II, better known as Dalavai Sethupathi, the Marava chieftain of Ramnad, was intending, for reasons unknown, to resign his throne in favour of an adopted son. One Tambi an illegitimate son of a deceased Sethupathi went to Madura, intrigued with the ministers and persuaded Tirumala to consent to oust the Dalavai and instal him on the gadi in his stead. Tirumala sent Tambi with an escort to Ramnad but then the Setupathi proved too strong for the feeble Tambi and refused so easily to vacate the throne. Tirumala made it a *casus bellum* to send a powerful army under Ramappaiya with orders to take Ramnad by storm. The Marava chieftain escaped to the Island of Rameswaram and entrenched himself behind a strongly fortified position. And while constructing a causeway to cross the channel between the island and the mainland, Ramappaiya suddenly died. His successor was, however, able to take the Sethupathi captive to Madura and confine him in prison there. We are unable to defend the conduct of Tirumala in the treatment that he gave to this loyal

Dalavai. It cannot be said that the Sethupathis had ever been disloyal or disobedient. On the other hand, they had rendered signal services to the State in many wars and in putting down revolts, particularly in the campaign against Tanjore and during a Mahomedan invasion from the north during the reign of Muthu Virappa Naik. They had administered their *poliams* energetically and with care and had won the love and esteem of their subjects. No emergency of State policy could have necessitated the humiliation of the Sethupathi; for as the subsequent events showed, the Tambi proved an incapable and unpopular weakling, and after some time Tirumala was forced to restore the Dalavai Setupathi to his ancient domain in the interests of the peace of the Marava country. In spite of this unprovoked aggression on the part of Tirumala, the Sethupathi continued to be a loyal and willing helper and gallantly saved Tirumala from the disgraceful plight to which he was reduced shortly afterwards, as the following narrative will show.

We now pass on to the last and greatest of the wars waged by Tirumala. This period of his reign was marked by plots and counter plots and schemes and intrigues scarcely paralleled in the whole of Indian History. The feeble emperor of Vijayanagar, during whose *regime* Tirumala had felt strong enough to revolt, was succeeded by a more powerful prince who at once determined to invade the south and reduce the refractory feudatories to submission. At the head of a large army he marched upon Gingee. Tirumala immediately formed a league with the Naiks of Tanjore and Gingee to oppose the imperial army. But the emperor succeeded in breaking up the league and isolating Tirumala from the others. Apprehending the dangerous situation into which he was thus placed, Tirumala resorted to the most unpatriotic and short-sighted expediency of seeking the help and protection of the Mahomedan Subhadar of Golconda. The southern march of the Imperial army was distracted by Mahomedan incursions in the northern frontiers and once more the Vijayanagar prince had to turn north to fight the Subha of Golconda. The war was long, tedious and indecisive. Finally Gingee was taken by the Mahomedans, who, flushed with victory, swooped down on Tanjore and Madura.

Tanjore submitted without a blow. But Tirumala caused a diversion by appealing to the king of Bijapur against his own ally who had now turned enemy. The embassy was successful and a large army was sent to Tirumala's help. But strange to say at the very hour of battle the Bijapur sepoys made common cause with their co-religionists of Golconda and reduced Tirumala to the greatest straits. Thus he was paid in his own coin and according to his deserts. Some respite was however granted to the hard stricken Tirumala by the assistance gallantly afforded by a battalion of the Vijayanagar troops. But everything was foiled shortly afterwards by a general insurrection among Tirumala's forces. Nothing was now left but to retreat to Madura and await there in dismay the development of events. The flood of Mahomedan invasion which had so long been kept back by the Vijayanagar empire now freely rolled over the south, spreading ruin and desolation in its march. At this juncture Tirumala's courage forsook him and he yielded up his capital without dealing a single blow in defence. A large sum of money was immediately paid to Bijapur for the expenses of the war and an annual tribute was promised.

Suddenly fortune turned in favor of the Emperor of Vijayanagar and lost grounds were rapidly recovered. In these campaigns the Mysoreans, who had ever been loyal to the Imperial house, rendered meritorious services. But once again the evil genius of Tirumala helped the Subhadar of Golconda to enter the Mysore territory and carry a war into that country. Nemesis was not long in coming, for, on their return, the Golconda troops plundered the city of Madura and carried away a large booty. Nor did the Raja of Mysore forget this act of ingratitude on the part of Tirumala. He invaded the Madura country and laid siege to the capital. Now at his wit's ends, Tirumala sought the aid of Sethupathi by sending him a most pitiable supplication in the name of his queen. The generous Sethupathi buried past grievances and responded to the call and Madura was saved.

Soon after this, Tirumala died in 1659 and a mystery envelops the manner of his death. We have said enough to correctly estimate his character and aims. Though it is unfair to detract from the posthumous glory of a man, history requires that the truth must be told. It may be contended that the skill, the art, and the taste displayed in the architectural monuments which he caused to be erected and which stand from generation to generation familiarising his name to the masses, point to a man of culture and refinement, but culture and refinement are not compatible with a 'hunt for noses' carried on during a Mysore campaign.

Tirumala was succeeded by his son, Muthu Alakadri, whose short reign of three years was marked by a Mahomedan invasion which swept as far south as Tanjore and Trichinopoly and which was finally bought off with a large sum of money. After the death of Alakadri, his son, Chokkanatha, a lad of 16 years, succeeded and immediately after his accession he led a campaign against the Mussulmans, in which however he was not very successful. But he was more successful in his war with Tanjore. Having fallen in love with a princess of the Tanjore Naiks, but having been refused her hand in marriage by the Tanjore Raja,

Muthu Alakadri 1659-62.

Chokkanatha, 1662-1682.

Chokkanatha made up his mind to accomplish by force what could not be gained by love. He, therefore, besieged Tanjore. The inmates of the palace performed Johur and the Raja died fighting with sword in hand. Chokkanatha appointed a Governor at Tanjore. But the very next year the Governor rebelled and became independent. A descendant of the old line had escaped and sought the protection of the Bijapur Sultan and the result was the expedition of Venkoji and the occupation of Tanjore by the Marathas.

A love incident.

Then followed an invasion of the country by the Mysoreans. The Marathas of Tanjore for the time being made common cause with Madura and succeeded in beating off the Mysore forces. Later on they themselves attacked Trichinopoly. At this unexpected treachery of an ally, it is said that Chokkanatha died of a broken heart.

His successor, Rangakrishna Muthuvirappa, though only a lad when he ascended the throne, did much to reconquer the lost possessions, recovered his capital, namely

Rangakrishna Muthuvirappa, 1982-89.

Trichinopoly, and restored the power of the Naiks to some of its former claims. Unfortunately he died of smallpox in 1689 at the very early age of 22. His young Queen, Muthammal, pregnant at the time, was with great difficulty persuaded to abstain from performing Sati until her delivery, after which, it is said that she drank rose water while in confinement and died of a fever that followed. The regency for this posthumous child was accepted and conducted with great skill and ability by Mangammal, the wife of Chokkanatha and the grandmother of the young child.

Vijiaranga Chokkanatha.

Like all great queens known to history, Mangammal was a woman of high spirit and bold enterprise. During her regency the Naik kingdom enjoyed peace and prosperity at home and won respect and glory abroad as much as it had done in the days of Tirumala or of the earlier kings. But to posterity Mangammal is better known as the founder of the many choultries and other charitable institutions which have sur-

The Regency of Mangammal, 1689—1704.

vived to the present day and lie scattered in all parts of the southern districts. All these still bear her name and some of them even lie outside her kingdom. She is said to have built many agraharams, villages, temples, tanks and wells. She is also said to have constructed well-paved roads and formed shady avenues connecting places of pilgrimage. A few of these exist and bear her name.

Different writers have suggested different motives for her charities and some of those suggested are not a little curious. One writer lays down that the charities were founded in expiation of youthful follies. Another less uncharitable writer repeats the popular story that in a moment of forgetfulness she put betel into her mouth with her left hand and this breach of a shastraic rule of conduct had to be patched up. There appears to be no need to invent stories to explain her motive for the charities. They were simply the result of individual disposition and national temperament. Poorhouses, water booths and the like are quite the common and popular forms of charity in India. A well known Maratha princess of Northern India of the following century chose exactly the same means of serving humanity and of perpetuating her own name thereby.

The first event of any political importance during the regency occurred in 1698. The Rajah of Travancore, who was a feudatory of the Naiks, had for some time past fallen into arrears in the payment of tribute. A small detachment of the Madura army was sent to enforce payment of the dues. The Rajah received the military visit with great cordiality and utilised the services of the army to get rid of his ministers who had usurped his power in the state. But when his purpose had been accomplished he fell upon the Naik force by surprise and dispersed and slaughtered it to a man. When the news of the unprovoked treachery of the vassal reached the ears of the Queen Regent, she immediately despatched another force under the able generalship of Narasappiah. He entered Travancore, reduced the recalcitrant feudatory to subjection and returned laden with a large booty of specie, jewels and guns.

About the year 1700, the Naik kingdom was embroiled in a war with the Maratha principality of Tanjore. During the campaign the armies of the rival powers lay for sometime encamped opposite to one another on the southern bank of the Cauvery, each waiting for the other to commence operations. Suddenly Narasappiah, the Brahmin general of the Naik army, hit upon a stratagem. He pretended a flank move on Tanjore. The Marathas saw that their capital was threatened and therefore broke up their camp and hurried to its defence, closely followed by the enemy. The Cauvery lay across in a high flood. The Marathas forded first and while doing so fell into disorder. Now was the opportunity of Narasappiah. Nor was he slow to seize it. He attacked the disorderly army of the enemy from the shore and gained a complete victory. The Tanjore prince sued for peace and bought it at a very high price.

Almost the next year these two neighbouring kingdoms entered into an offensive alliance against the Rajah of Mysore and made preparations for the invasion of his kingdom. The cause of the intended attack seems to have been that the Rajah of Mysore had built a dam across the Cauvery and diverted the water to the great detriment of the arable lands round about Trichinopoly and Tanjore. But before any invasion took place a heavy flood came down the river and carried away the dam and so removed the *casus bellum.*

In 1702, the country suffered a great loss by the death of Narasappiah, the trusted minister and general of Mangammal, in a skirmish with the Sethupathi of Ramnad. The Jesuit missionaries of the time, no friendly critics of the Brahmin minister, speak of him as the greatest without exception of the ministers who guided the affairs of the Naik kingdom.

In 1704, the ward came of age and this event led to the formation of political factions in the capital hostile to Mangammal. The aged Queen Regent withdrew from the capital and seems to have spent the remaining days of her life in her palace at Madura in quiet retirement.

Nelson's version of the retirement of the Queen Regent is different. He says that she scandalised the court by her love for her minister and as a result she was imprisoned in her own palace at Madura and cruelly starved to death. He admits that there is no authentic record for this story and that it is only based on an oral tradition. However he has tried to find corroborative evidence. He says "there is nothing prima facie improbable in it as it stands, and there exists some evidence tending to corroborate it. A statue of a young man may be seen in the little chapel built by Mangammal on the west side of the Golden Lily Tank, which is commonly known as the statue of Mangammal's minister and paramour [Achchiah the successor of Narasappiah] and in a picture on the ceiling of the chapel there is a portrait of the same person opposite to one of the queen, and it is observable that the portrait of Mangammal shows that she did not dress as an orthodox widow would dress and indulged in jewels and finery fit only for a married woman. These circumstances are certainly in favour of the story of the intrigue with Achchiah being true; and if so, then the story of the imprisonment and murder is rendered more worthy of credence." We are constrained to state that Nelson's evidence fails to corroborate the tradition. He appears to have totally misread the representations in figure as also the writing in the chapel. Besides, there are many inconsistencies in his version which will have to be explained before his view can be accepted. The most apparent is that at the time of which Nelson is speaking Mangammal was at least 50 years of age and well past love-making. Oral tradition is sometimes very misleading and has to be carefully scrutinized before acceptance.

Vijiaranga Chokkanatha 1704-1731.

After the demise of Mangammal in 1704 A. D. her grandson and ward Vijiaranga Chokkanatha ascended the throne. His feeble and dull rule extended over a period of 26 years, which he spent mostly in touring from one place of pilgrimage to another, lavishing large gifts on them. A dispute about the succession to the masnad of Ramnad led to the interference of Chokkanatha and the Tanjore prince and to the final division of that part of the country into Sivaganga and Ramnad, a division which has ever since remained so. This pious prince died in 1731.

Minakshi rules, 1731-1736.

His Queen, Minakshi, assumed the reins of government and adopted a young boy, son of Bangaru Tirumala. A year or two later Bangaru Tirumala rose in rebellion and claimed to act as regent and appealed to Safdar Ali, the son and heir-apparent of the Nawab of the Carnatic. Minakshi sought the assistance of his brother-in-law, the famous Chanda Saheb, who figures so prominently in the wars of the Carnatic. Tirumala was ousted and driven off to the South. But the friendly ally of Minakshi soon showed a hostile attitude and himself occupied the city of Trichinopoly, threw Minakshi into prison and usurped the government.

Usurpation of Chanda Saheb.

The unfortunate queen, the last of the Naiks, took poison and put an end to her life. Thus ended the Naik rule at Madura in 1736. A few families in Sivaganga claim to be the descendants and receive state pensions.

Death of Minakshi.

Whether the country at large profited or no by their rule, the city of Madura did to a great extent and owes to them the present arrangement of its streets, its

Benefits of the Naik rule at Madura.

general plan, its buildings, a flourishing industrial community and its general prosperity.

We may very briefly pass over the events that followed. Chanda Saheb ruled in Trichinopoly till 1740, when he was captured by the Marathas, who appointed Murari Rau Governor of Trichinopoly and Madura. In 1743, the Nizam once more restored the Mussalman authority and appointed Anwar-uddin Nawab of the Carnatic. Madura and Tinnevelly remained in the hands of Mahomed Ali, his son, during the Carnatic wars. In 1751 one Alam Khan an adherent of the enemy occupied Madura. An attempt made by Mahomed Ali, with the assistance of Captain Cope, to take Madura by storm failed disastrously and the forces deserted at the time of need to the enemy. In 1755, Mahomed Ali sent another expedition under the command of the English leader, Col. Heron, Mahfuz Khan (Mahomed Ali's elder brother) and Yusuf Khan. This expedition was more successful than the first. They occupied Madura. The district was rented to Mahfuz

Mahomedans once more at Madura.

Heron's' Expedition 1755.

Khan whose administration, however, was a complete failure. He was not able to collect the stipulated revenue or to pay the salaries of the sepoys and soldiers of the East India Company stationed for his protection. So Yusuf Khan was sent to replace him.

Mahfuz appointed to collect the rents.

Mahfuz rebelled. Yusuf could do nothing until help arrived from Trichinopoly under the command of Captain Caillaud. This officer attempted a night attack on the fort of Madura near the west gate but at the critical moment the whole plan was frustrated by the barking of a dog which had followed the raiding party. Another attempt was equally unsuccessful. The fort was however finally handed over to Captain Caillaud on receipt of a large sum of money by the rebels.

Capt. Caillaud fails to take Madura.

On the occupation of the fort, Yusuf Khan was granted the right to collect the revenues. In a few years owing to some differences of opinion, he also rebelled, held out the fortress and repelled an attack. But at last he was treacherously captured by a French Officer and

Yusuf appointed to collect the rents.

His early life and character.

handed over to the East India Company. He was promptly executed by the English. His tomb is marked by a mosque near the toll gate on the road leading from Madura to Dindigul. Born of a Vellala caste in the Ramnad country, Yusuf Khan Saheb, better known as the Khansa, left his home while still very young; served a European in Pondicherry; came into the favour and notice of the Nawab of Arcot; then he entered the army and was afterwards appointed to the command of all the sepoy forces of the East India Company. We have seen him appointed to collect the revenues of Madura and undergoing unmerited execution. "His whole administration denoted vigour and effect. His justice was unquestioned, his word unalterable. His measures were happily combined and firmly executed. During his regime the guilty had no refuge from punishment."

Madura handed over to E. I. Co.

In 1781, the revenues of the Carnatic were assigned by Mahomed Ali to the East India Company to defray the expenses of the second Mysore war and thenceforward the Company appointed their own officers to collect the revenue. The first to be so appointed was George Proctor. This agreement came to an end in 1785. In 1790 the Madras Government, in return for debt due to them, took possession of the country by proclamation without treaty. In 1801 an agreement was made by which the Nawab of Arcot handed over to the East India Company in perpetuity "the sole and exclusive administration of the civil and military government of all the territories and dependencies of the Carnatic." Thus Madura finally came into the hands of the English.

The Genealogy of the Naik Kings of Madura.

I. Nagama Naik—1559.

II. Visvanatha Naik—1559-1563.

III. Kumara Krishnappa—1563-1573 *alias* Peria Krishnama.

IV. Krishnappa or Peria Virappa—1573-1595 * V. Visvanatha II—1573-1595 *

(Sons of IV:) VI. Lingayya *alias* Kumara Krishnappa—1595-1602. VII. Visvappa *alias* Visvanath III—1595-1602.

VIII. Muthu Krishnappa—1602-1609.

(Sons of VIII:) IX. Muthu Virappa—1609-1623. X. Tirumala—1623-1659. Kumaramuthu.

XI. Muthu Alakadri—1659-1662.

XII. Chokkanatha—1662-1682.
= XIV. Mangammal Regent—1689-1704,

XIII. Rangakrishna Muthu Virappa—1682-1689.

XV. Vijiaranga Chokkanath—1704-1731.
= XVI. Minakshi—1731-1736.

* Joint rule.

THE MINAKSHI TEMPLE.

INTRODUCTION.

The temple of Minakshi occupying the heart of the city and forming the nucleus around which the streets are arranged is by far the greatest attraction of the place. The name of Madura is in the minds of Indians inseparably associated with the temple of Minakshi and there are few throughout the length and breadth of the land who have not heard of the fame of the Goddess Minakshi. That name may be heard on the lips of country girls mentioned in the same breath with the deities of Kanchi, holy Kasi and Ramesvaram. The silent influence exerted by this great centre of religion on the life of the people is incalculable and any one who aspires to have an insight into the life and aspirations of the Hindus must visit the great temple. It is in a way the outward embodiment of the civilization and culture of the Hindu race. There within the four walls of the temple one finds all that is best and highest in the civilization of the Hindus—particularly the Tamils of

The God and Goddess of the Temple, Madura.

From a Photo by J. W. H. Joshua, Madura.

of Southern India. Their highest achievements in literature, science and arts have been in the service of their Gods. Even at the present day the temple is a means of educating the masses. The Hindu populace derives from there the knowledge of its Gods, its philosophy and its Pauranic history. It is also from there that it imbibes its ideals of life and conduct. Its festivals attract thousands of country folk from the neighbouring villages and help to keep alive the sense of the solidarity of the Hindu nationality in the midst of the diversity of its castes and creeds. The temple affords the means of livelihood to hundreds of the inhabitants of the city. It extends its patronage to artisans, painters, architects, musicians, bhagavathars and to men learned in the sacred lore, and does at the present day for the improvement of the fine arts what the kings did in olden times. Its gates are ever open to the poor and the homeless. It is the one ever hospitable asylum to the wandering gosain as well as the local mendicant. To the pious and the afflicted it is the source of divine consolation.

The influence of the temple on the past history and fortunes of the city is in no less degree marked. In the earliest days the town derived its name of Nanmadakudal from the splendour of the towers of the temple.* As has been mentioned already, Siva himself is said to have given it the name of Madura. The abode of the deity is the stronghold of the Brahmans and formed the rallying ground for Saivism against the attacks of Jainism, Buddhism and against the activities of the Jesuit missionaries in the 17th century. On more than one occasion the temple was the cause, miraculous or otherwise, of arresting the waning prosperity of the city and setting it on a new course of development. On more than one occasion it also shared the misfortunes that betook the city. Its stone walls still bear the marks of gunshot and the mutilation of a few of its images point to the hand of the infidel. Between 1736 and 1740, while the city was under the occupation of the Mahomedans, the temple was closed until the Marathas came to its help. Some of the great men who figure in the history of the city have been closely connected with the

---

* Nanmadakudal or more briefly, Kudal, is the name by which Madura is known in the earlier classics. The word means a cluster of four towers.

growth of the temple. Princes and nobles vied with one another in propitiating the deity. Tirumala, Aryanatha, Viravasanta, Minakshi Naik and even Rouse Peter of living memory made large endowments to the temple, and in doing so unconsciously perpetuated their own names.

The architecture of the temple.

Before proceeding to describe in detail the different parts of the temple it may be well to say a few words about its architecture generally. The shape and structure of the temple has undergone change several times in the past. No part of the present edifice can be said to be older than the beginning of the 16th century. Therefore it represents the later style of Dravidian religious architecture. Fergusson, the great authority on Indian and Eastern architecture, rightly says "it possesses all the characteristics of a first class Dravidian temple"—the characteristics being lofty pyramidal towers dominating the surrounding landscape; rectangular enclosures one within the other like a china box; a multitude of cloisters, galleries and porches; delicate sculpture worked on ponderous material; the use of the horizontal roofing and the entire absence of the dome or the arch. The material used in construction is stone, and timber has been completely excluded (except in the upper galleries of the towers where it was used surreptitiously). The temple is almost a regular rectangle, measuring 750 feet by 830 feet, covering an area of 25 acres, and is enclosed by four high stone walls each of which is pierced by a gopuram or pyramidal tower. The central shrines of Minakshi and her divine consort Chokkanatha or Sundaresvara are surrounded by three enclosures and each of these is protected by four minor towers at the four points of the compass, the outer tower growing larger and reaching higher than the corresponding inner one. In front of Minakshi's shrine is the Golden Lily Tank. The temple also contains a Hall of Thousand Columns, a Hall of Silver or Velliambalam, a sanctuary for the sixty-three Nayanars or Saivite saints, another for the Sangathars, the fellows of the ancient Tamil academy. Space is also provided for a large number of small shrines for the minor deities and a multitude of mantapams, cloisters, galleries, store houses, kitchens and flower gardens, all necessary for the proper upkeep of the sacred temple. Innumerable figures, statues of princes and saints, bas-reliefs, scenes from the sacred chronicle either worked on stone or roughly painted on walls are met with in various parts of the building. Details of ornamentation are also found on the capitals and shafts of columns, basements of turrets, and on the eaves and corners of the stone roofing. Some of these will be described in detail later.

In describing the temple the writer of the District Gazetteer, on the authority of some general observations made by Fergusson in his "History of Indian and Eastern Architecture," says that the temple is an aimless aggregate of parts that seem to have been added as time and circumstances dictated during a long course of time rather than in accordance with the requirements of a deliberately set plan and hence it lacks unity of plan and fails in effect. It is doubtful if Fergusson meant to apply his general remarks on South Indian temples to the Minakshi temple in particular. He himself admits that he could not get any copy of a ground plan of the temple. It is unfortunate that sound and sufficient knowledge and the right attitude of mind are not brought to bear on the study and criticism of the Indian arts. Unquestioning obedience to authority is still the order of the day in matters of art criticism in India. That the temple grew up by parts and during a long period of time is quite true. Indeed it could not have been otherwise. But to say that it is an aimless aggregate of parts without any plan and that it therefore lacks unity and fails in effect is a direct contradiction of facts. A study of the ground plan is sufficient to disprove the statement made above owing to deficient knowledge. In the first place, the seat of the chief deity is exactly at the point of intersection of the straight lines joining the pairs of opposite towers. One happy effect of this central situation is that the Vimana or golden top of the central shrine is seen from a great distance in the west through the apertures of two successive towers. Secondly, the area covered by the shrine of the God is exactly a fourth of the area of the temple and that of the shrine of the Goddess exactly one fourth the area of the shrine of the God. Thirdly, each of the shrines is enclosed in two prakarams and both together in a larger one. This arrangement serves a special purpose. It is enjoined in the Hindu sastras that the devotee shall, before worshipping the deity, go round him three times. People generally do this by walking round the length of the enclosure three times in temples where there is only one enclosure. In the Madura temple a walk along each of the prakarams makes up the heaven-appointed triple round. Fourthly, the distribution of the minor towers in the temple can scarcely be said to be aimless. They are located in particular points of a geometrical figure. Even in the matter of height such a gradation was adopted as would produce the most pleasing effect. The view presented by the cluster of these towers starting from the central Vimana and rising in a gallery one above another, until at last the last of the series seems almost to reach the skies, is most superb and is a favourite subject of Indian and European painters. This view is best obtained from the eastern arcade of the Golden Lily Tank. The store houses, kitchens and cloisters are so hidden away that a stranger cannot at first sight detect them, and the one or two stray pavilions that do not fit in with the general plan are so few in number that they in no way interfere with the unity or mar the effect of the whole.

Not admitting its validity, one can well understand the criticism. It appears to be due to lack of closer study. The temple is so large, so elaborate, so much diversified in detail, that the plan and unity of structure are not apparent at first sight. But this need not, and ought not to, detract from its claims to high artistic merit. Some of the world's greatest masterpieces of poetry, music, painting and sculpture, which were on first appearance condemned on superficial observation, have been declared later by competent judges to possess the highest excellence.

Again, the criticism that South Indian temples are disappointing by the insignificance of the central part and the simplicity of the innermost shrine, although they are very imposing from a distance on account of their colossal towers, appears to be due to a difference in ideals. The critics believe that the most important part should be the grandest. The ideal of the builders seems to have been the reverse The pious devotee coming from the outside world, with all its vain pomp and glory, is agreeably surprised by the huge towers, but as he enters the pagoda and crosses prakaram after prakaram, he gradually loses sight of the ephemeral world outside till at last in the innermost sanctuary in the holy of the holies, standing before the deity in an atmosphere of burning incense, sacred ashes, and the sweet smell of flowers and sandal, and in the sombre lamplight, he is lost in contemplation and is in communion with the Supreme Spirit. Such appears to have been the effect intended by the ancient builders and designers of the sacred temple.

The Hindus are an essentially religious people. They are more idealistic than realistic, and their ideals are drawn from their philosophy and their religion. These facts have to be constantly kept in mind in the study of their arts, literature and institutions. Failure to understand and assume this point of view has led even the most impartial of Western critics into many serious misconceptions of Hindu thought and life, and has deprived them of one very useful key to the mysteries of the apparently grotesque East, its systems, their workings, aims and purposes.

Assuming for a while the rôle of a guide, let us lead the tourist from the railway station towards the western tower. This is the most graceful of all the towers, the tapering upwards being most gradual. From an oblong basement of sculptured stone, it rises in a pyramidal shape into a gallery of nine storys. At the top it ends in a cylindrical form lying horizontally. It is indented all round by a number of bays and balconies and is profusely covered with plaster figures depicting in relief scenes from the epics and puranas. The upper storys are built of brick and chunam. Its height above the ground is about 150 feet.

The western tower.

The temple wall is protected from pollution and is kept in good condition by a neat garden laid out around it and fenced in by iron railings. It is said that the garden was laid out and enclosed in the eighties of the last century by Mr. Crole, a Collector of the district. Driving round the Chitrai Street, we next come upon the Mottai gopuram or the peakless tower, so called from the incomplete condition in which it long remained until recently the charity of the Chetties gave a finishing touch

South Tower of the Temple, Madura.

From a Photo by J. W. H. Joshua, Madura.

to the upper storys and the summit. It is the plainest of the towers, containing only a few figures. At the foot of this tower in a niche resides Mottai gopurathan, the Guardian Deity of the Northern Tower—an easily irritable and fierce God. He is a favourite with the lower castes and is reputed to be particularly fond of young women. A safe child-birth, a marriage, a recovery from cholera or any other epidemic disease are occasions for people living in these quarters of the town to propitiate him with the sacrifice of goats and fowls and pongal (rice cooked with jaggery and spices). A common votive offering to him is the garlanding of the whole tower—not an impossible task. Passing onwards, we arrive at the eastern tower. It closely resembles the Chidambaram tower in bulk and proportions, and contains a few inscriptions not yet deciphered. At the foot of this tower is the Madurai Veeran, the Guardian Deity of Madura. He is also feared very much by credulous people and is propitiated at times with hundreds of pots of sandal paste.

The peakless tower.

Madurai Veeran.

By the side of Madurai Veeran is the Pathinettampadi or the Eighteen steps. The platform above this gallery is the place where oaths are sworn by disputants and credulous country folk believe that a lie uttered at this spot is visited with immediate death.

Going farther southwards the temple is entered in front of the Goddess' shrine by a vaulted porch known as the Ashtasakthi mantapam (the porch of the eight powers), so called from the representation on the ceiling in plaster figures of the local deity in her eight different forms. Both sides of the porch are occupied by bazaars where cocoanuts, plantains, camphor and other things necessary for offering at the temple are sold. At the end of the porch, guarding the gateways, there stand on both sides two good-sized monolithic images of the sons of Siva—Ganesa and Subramanya. These deities are seen almost at every entrance throughout the temple.

Ganesa.

Of these two deities Ganesa was born to Parvathi, the wife of Siva, out of her scurf. He is represented as short, stout, with a protuberant belly, an elephant's head and only one tusk and four

Front Entrance to the Shrine of the Temple, Madura.

From a Photo by J. W. H. Joshua, Madura.

hands holding in them a shell, a discus, a club, and a waterlily. His vahanam (vehicle) is the mouse. Legends account for his elephant's head by the story that his mother Parvathi, proud of her son, asked Sani (Saturn) to look upon him, forgetful of the well-known evil effects of Sani's glance. He turned to see the beautiful boy and the boy's head was burnt to ashes instantly. Brahma, the creator, took compassion on the bereaved mother and commanded her to cut off the head of any man, woman or beast that she could find handy and place it on the body of Ganesa. Parvathi happened to find an elephant first in her search and thus came Ganesa to bear an elephant's head. Another version of the story is that Parvathi having gone in to bathe, left her son to guard the entrance. Siva arrived and challenged admission; and Ganesa refusing, a fight ensued and resulted in the loss of Ganesa's head. In order to pacify the angry mother, Siva immediately replaced it with that of an elephant as it was the first that came to hand. And here is the story about his single tusk. Parasurama, the destroyer of the Kshatriyas, once called at Siva's residence, and finding Ganesa at the gateway, asked to be admitted.

As Siva was then sleeping, Ganesa could not grant the request. Parasurama became angry and displayed his warlike inclinations. Ganesa caught him with his trunk, whirled him in the sky and left him senseless on the ground. However, recovering consciousness in a short time, Parasurama hurled his 'parasu' or battle-axe at Ganesa. Now this axe had been obtained by Parasurama as a gift from Siva for the performance of a severe penance. Knowing it therefore to be his father's weapon Ganesa respectfully received it on one of his tusks which it splintered. And henceforth Ganesa became Ekadanta, the single tusked. Ganesa is also the God of wisdom, having written down the whole of the Mahabharata—the great Epic of the Hindus—to the dictation of Vyasa. To-day Ganesa is chiefly worshiped as the Remover of obstacles and no Hindu fails to invoke his aid at the commencement of any undertaking, great or small.

Subramanya.

Just as Ganesa emerged from Parvathi's body so did Subramanya from that of her Lord Siva. Subramanya is the generalissimo of the Gods in their wars against the asuras. He was fostered by the Pleiades and therefore bears the other name of Kartikeya. He is represented with 6 heads, 12 hands holding bows and arrows and riding the peacock. It is the birth of this war-god that is narrated with such dramatic skill and poetic beauty by the great sanskrit poet and dramatist Kalidasa in his famous lyric of Kumara Sambhava.

With the permission of the Remover of Obstacles and the Rider of the Peacock, we enter a large five-aisled mantapam supported on six rows of stone pillars. The central aisle is very broad and high. The architectural device to shorten the width of the roof by the introduction of projecting lions over the capitals of pillars is worth noticing here. The Mantapam is said to have been built by Minakshi Naik, one of the ministers of Tirumala, and is therefore named after him. The remaining two aisles on either side are occupied by bazaars where sweets, flowers, and toilet articles are sold. The outer aisles are used as stables for the temple elephants, five or six of which are always maintained from the temple revenues for use during processions. At the other end of the aisle leading into the inner prakaram is a fine, tall, brass archway called Tiruvachi, containing hundreds of small oil lamps which are lighted at sunset every day. The illumination is grand and is visible from a long distance. The brass frame work was presented to the temple by a former Zemindar of Sivaganga and its upkeep has been provided for by the grant of villages.

Turning to the left we enter the outermost prakaram or enclosure called the 'Audiveedi.' It is well paved with stones and kept quite clean. The southern and western sides are respectively occupied by the Minakshi and Alagar Koil Devasthanams or temple offices. The shrine is entered by the gate leading from the southern tower. It opens upon the Golden Lily Tank which is surrounded on the four sides by arcades. The tank yields no lilies at present, but in mythical times it furnished flowers to Indra during his sojourn on the earth. This accounts for its name. One peculiar feature of the tank is that it breeds no fish. Mythology has it that once upon a time a crane was performing penance by the side of the tank and the fat fishes swimming in the tank tempted it. But it resisted the

The Golden Lily Tank, Western side; inside the Temple, Madura

From a Photo by J. W. H. Joshua, Madura.

temptation and when it attained *mukti* (liberation), one of the boons it sought of God was that the tank should contain no animal life ever more. The walls of the arcades are covered with fresco painting of a very inferior quality, illustrating stories from the local chronicle. The view of the temple from the eastern arcade is one of the most beautiful sights. It opens out a panorama of ascending towers and glittering canopies interspersed with cocoanut palms. To realise the utility of this tank to the orthodox Hindu, one has to visit it between the hours of 5 and 7 in the evening, when hundreds of Brahmans are seen performing their evening ablutions to the chant of the Vedic hymns. The arcades are filled with students of the Sanskrit and Vedic schools attached to the temple reciting their texts. On its banks might be seen old pundits explaining the Ramayana, the Mahabharata or other ancient classics to listening crowds of pious people. A plunge in the tank is the surest way to heaven. The Mahatmya asserts how a bath in the tank obtained for Indra freedom from the sin of Brahman slaughter, one of the five great sins according to the Hindu Sastras.

Projecting into the tank are a balcony and a porch of polished black marble in front of it, said to have been built by the famous Queen Regent of Madura, Mangammal. The porch is used as the seat of the deity during one of the festivals. On the ceiling of the balcony can be seen painted the figures of Mangammal, her grandson Chokkanatha, and Ramayyan Dalavai, the famous general of Tirumala. From the granite porch, the hall leads on to the Kilikatti Mantapam, so called from the cages of parrots hanging there. Attached to the pillars supporting the pavilion are figures of Vali and Sugriva and the Pancha Pandavas. On either side of the entrance to Minakshi's shrine are the sanctuaries of Ganesa and Subramanya. A large number of cocoanuts are offered every day to Ganesa. It ought to be stated here that Europeans are not permitted farther inside. We now cross the entrance and pass into the inner prakaram of the Goddess' shrine. The only thing of especial interest in the inner prakaram is a beautiful life-size figure of Tirumala Naik at the southern extremity of the eastern corridor. Next we enter the innermost prakaram. The walls of the corridors in this prakaram are fully decorated with paintings of scenes from the Periyapuranam recording the lives of the 63 Saivite saints. The ceiling is also covered with paintings of lotuses; though the art displayed may not be of the first rank, the labour of painting the ceiling lying on one's back must indeed have been very exacting. Thence we enter the innermost sanctuary which is sacred to Minakshi (literally, the fish-eyed) and now we are in her immediate presence.

The story of Minakshi.

As we have already said, Minakshi is Parvathi in another form. Once upon a time there ruled in the Pandya country a king called Malayadhwaja. He was childless for a long time, and fearing the possible extinction of his family, he performed a great sacrifice, and in recompense for his arduous penance, by the grace of Siva, Parvathi herself appeared from the sacrificial fire in the form of a child. Though overjoyed at the gift, the royal parents were concerned to see that the girl had three breasts. But an angel soon appeared before them and said that the third breast would disappear when she found her husband. Time passed and the girl came of age. The royal parents died, thus making her Queen of Madura before her time. Shortly after, she started on a conquering expedition and subdued all earthly princes and heavenly deities not excepting Indra. And when at last she encountered Siva, her third breast disappeared suddenly, and lo! she was in the presence of her future lord. Then follows the story of their love and finally Siva comes down to Madura as Sundara Pandya, marries her and reigns as the King of Madura. After ruling for a long time and after anointing the crown prince as his successor, Parvathi and Paramesvara cast off their mortal coils and once more resume their sacred abode in the temple as Sundaresvara and Minakshi.

Having worshipped Minakshi, in her graceful presence, we take leave of her and pass along to Chandikesvara. We are enjoined to take leave formally of this gentleman before we quit the Goddess' shrine. He is in deep penance and you attract his attention by a clap of hands. Back again in the Kilikatti Mantapam, we pass along northward and enter the outer enclosure of Siva's shrine by the southern gate. As we step in, just in front, is the Mukkuruni Pillayar, a great monolithic figure of Ganesa. On his birthday every year, and on special occasions, he is offered a stupendous pudding made of 18 measures of pounded rice. This fact gives him his name of Mukkuruni Pillayar. This image is said to have been discovered while the great tank to the east of Madura was excavated. The Mukkuruni Pillayar is seated in a position where he can be seen from a great distance along the southern tower street through the entrance in the tower. Tradition has it that behind him in the temple wall there was an aperture opening into the shrine and that the figure Sabhapathi within (Siva in his dancing attitude) could be seen from a great distance from outside the temple. The fierceness of the glance of Nataraja, the King of Dancers, was such that it burnt every object that it fell upon and so great was the havoc committed in the southern part of Madura that this opening was closed and the great figure of Ganesa was interposed as an effective obstruction. Tradition also has it that from that day forward there was no house-burning nor loss of life in that part of the city. With the permission of the Lord of three Kurunis, we walk up the three corridors of the enclosure. They are high, broad and well-lit at present, though neither so long, nor so high as those of the famous Ramesvaram temple. The entrance to the God's inner enclosure is guarded by four huge guardians of the gateway—two inside and two outside. Those inside are said to be the figures of two kings of Madura. Close by these two figures there are some stone inscriptions and they do not appear to have been deciphered yet. The southern corridor of the inner prakaram contains the stone figures of the 63 Saivite saints of Southern India. Their lives and doings are recorded in the Tamil classic called Periapuranam. At the further end is the sanctuary of Dakshinamoorthy and a pavilion for the utsava vigrahas. The northern extremity of the western corridor is occupied by a choice collection of marble figures representing all the idols in the famous temple of Visvanath in holy Kasi, Benares. They are said to have been presented to the temple by a late Raja of Benares during one of his tours of pilgrimage in Southern India. Here is also the sanctuary of Ellam Valla Siddhar—the Seer

The God's shrine.

Ellam Valla Siddhar.

that can conquer everything. In one of his avatars Sundaresvara appeared in Madura as a saint performing wonderful miracles, making the old young, the blind to see, the deaf to hear, and the lame to walk; and his fame spread far and wide. It reached the ears of the king and he was instantly summoned to the royal palace, but the saint would not come as he had to do little with earthly monarchs. Some time later the king and the saint met accidentally in the temple and the king derisively asked him whether, in proof of his great powers, he could make a stone elephant eat a sugar-cane. And the story goes that to the great surprise and consternation of the King the stone elephant not only ate the sugar-cane stretched up to it but put forth its proboscis to take the pearl necklace from the king's neck The king immediately fell at the feet of the saint and apologised for his bad manners. And a shrine was built then and there in honour of the saint. Even now, year after year, the event is celebrated in a fitting manner, and no lord in all the temple grants boons so readily as does Ellam Valla Siddhar to whom all is possible.

Close by is a niche set apart for Durga, and opposed to the fierce goddess stands the stump of an old tree said to be the only relic of the ancient forest of Kadamba which occupied the modern site of Madura. It is preserved with great care, and every devotee touches it and places his hands on his eyes in token of his veneration for the relic. Further on is the Sakshi Kinaru—the well that bore witness. A certain merchant living in a village near Madura was blessed with a handsome daughter as the reward of a great penance, and he intended to give her in marriage to his nephew in the town. But before the girl came of age the parent died. On hearing of the death the nephew went to the village, took possession of the property and his fair cousin and set out homeward to Madura. On the way he was bitten by a snake and died. The unhappy girl's lamentations were heard by Tirugnana Sambandha Murthi, a Saivite saint, who happened to pass by, and he took pity on her and by his miraculous powers restored her lover to life and had them married then and there in the presence of a linga and a well. But the bridegroom had been already married to an-

Tha Kadamba Relic.

other woman. The couple arrived at Madura and the two wives lived peacefully together for some time, but eventually quarrels arose. The first wife demanded what evidence there was to prove that the second had been legitimately married. And the latter implored God Sundaresvara for help and performed a severe penance. Always gracious to the helpless, God Sundaresvara granted that the linga and the well on the wayside should go to Madura and bear witness to her marriage. They did so, and have ever since remained in the Madura temple.

Natesa.

From the innermost prakaram we enter the court-yard in front of the Holy of Holies. On the right hand side is the dancing figure of Natesa. He is otherwise known as Sabhapathi. His abode is called the Velliambalam, the Hall of Silver, as contrasted with the one at Chidambaram called the Ponnambalam or the Hall of Gold. The large figure is plated with silver and is one of the grandest in the temple. He is none other than Siva in his dancing attitude—a posture that he assumed in his ecstatic moments, and you come across this form of

Siva very frequently in the temple. The traditional story is that when Siva came to the earth in the form of Sundara Pandya and married the princess Minakshi, just as the wedding-party were proceeding to dinner, Patanjali and Vyāgrapātha, two rishis who had come to attend the marriage, would not share the repast without previously witnessing the dance of Siva, as was their custom; whereupon Siva immediately gratified their desire by dancing. But it is noticeable that, whereas in other places of sanctity he dances on the right leg with the left pointing up, here he dances on his left leg and his right leg points to the sky. The Sacred Chronicle gives the following explanation of the peculiarity. One of the later Pandyas was a great devotee of Siva and was learned in the 63 arts. While conversing with a visitor from the Chola country he discovered to his mortification that he had not learnt the one remaining art of dancing in which the Chola King, his rival, was an adept, and immediately set to learn it. He found the exercises so difficult and taxing that he wondered how Siva could dance without even once changing his legs for all time, and so much was he filled with compassion for the deity that one night he entered the temple undiscovered, and after all the doors had been closed for the night, prostrated himself before the God and prayed that he might change his legs or he would kill himself as a sacrifice. The God was so much pleased with the devotion of the prince that he granted his request and changed his legs. At the entrance to the sanctuary of Natesa are the statues of the two rishis, Patanjali and Vyāgrapātha, referred to above. The former of these is the famous author of the Bhashyas or Commentaries on Panini's Sanskrit Grammar. He is also the author of a short treatise on Yoga which superseded all the earlier and voluminous works on that system of philosophy. Of the minor deities in front of Natesa the most conspicuous are the old lady with 60 children and Chitragupta, minister of the Lord of Death and Recorder and Accountant-General of men's merits and sins.

The Holy of Holies.

Passing onward into the interior you enter the Holy of Holies. This is a beautiful small shrine—a Vimana supported by eight elephants and covered by a golden canopy. It stands quite separately by itself, surrounded by a small moat, and displays an unequalled unity and finish of execution. As a piece of architecture it is a gem and is well worthy of the reputation of having descended from Mount Kailas, the abode of Siva. The image of Siva in the form of a linga is placed in the centre of the shrine, and here he bears the name of Sundaresvara.

Sundaresvara.

It may here be mentioned that Siva is the third member of the Hindu Triad, the other two being Brahma and Vishnu. As Brahma is the creator, and Vishnu, the preserver, so is Siva the destroyer of all, and as such he is known by the names of Rudra and Mahakala. But destruction in Hindu belief implies reproduction. So, as Siva or Sankara, he is the reproductive power which is perpetually restoring that which has been dissolved. Under this character, he is represented as a linga. He is Isvara, the lord of all. He is also the Mahayogi, the naked ascetic Digambara. He is Bhutesvara, lord of all spirits, and so haunts cemeteries and crematoriums, wearing serpents round his head and body, skulls for a necklace, his body besmeared with ashes, attended by troops of imps and trampling upon rebellious demons. He sometimes indulges in revelry, and, heated with drink, dances furiously with his wife Devi, the dance called Tandava, surrounded by hosts of dancing attendants. He is three-eyed, the third eye, the eye of wisdom and wrath, being in the centre of the forehead. He is blue-throated, because of the deadly poison he swallowed in order to save the world. He is five-faced and four-armed. His third eye is surmounted by the moon's crest. His matted locks are gathered up into a coil which contains the river Ganga, whom he caught as she rushed down from heaven with irresistible force. In his hand he holds a trisula or trident called Pinaka. His garment is the skin of a deer. Occasionally he is seated on a tiger skin and holds a deer in his hand. His attendant is Nandi, the Bull. His bow is Ajagava ; his drum, damaru ; his club, khatvaga ; his noose or chord, pasa. His abode is in Kailasa. Throughout the temple are scattered many figures representing Siva in his various forms.

Taking leave of Sundaresvara we retrace our steps and arrive at the entrance to the second enclosure. Immediately on the left is Dandayudapani, the God of Palni—Subramanya in the form of an ascetic—and farther on are the figures of the nine planets no two of which face each other. In front of the entrance are Nandi, the Sacred Bull, and the flagstaff in a beautiful mantapam called the Kambattadi Mantapam. The carving on the pillars supporting this mantapam is most superb. It is one of the finest sights of the temple. The workmanship is so fine, the chiselling so delicate, and on such untractable material too, that one is lost in silent admiration for the artist.

Ravana under Kailas.

Particularly among these figures may be noted a bas relief on the south-western pillar representing Ravana in a penance with Mount Kailas on his back—Ravana, the ten-headed monster, the Lord of Lanka and the enemy of Rama. This Rakshasa once took it into his head to carry off Mount Kailas, with Parvathi and Paramesvara in order to deck his own capital, and with this desire he proceeded north and reached the Himalayas. After lifting the hill on his back, not without much difficulty, and as he was preparing to start homeward, he felt a sudden weight crushing him down. The lifting of the hill had caused a shock and frightened Parvathi and she ran and embraced her lord, seeking protection. Paramesvara divined the situation in an instant and pressed the hill with his left toe, intending to teach a lesson to the audacious Rakshasa. Ravana, crestfallen and caught under without any way of escape, sought for mercy, reciting with great humility the sacred and soul-stirring songs of the Samaveda to the accompaniment of the veena, himself playing upon it with his twenty hands. The great lord Paramesvara was pleased, as who would not be, and thought fit, in his divine mercy, to liberate the repenting Rakshasa.

The nobility of conception of this myth is in this piece of sculpture only matched by the grandeur of its execution. Details are worked in without in the least marring the effect of the whole. The Kailas with Parvathi and Paramesvara and all their heavenly attendants, and Ravana underneath supporting the hill on his ten heads and playing upon the veena with his twenty hands in a kneeling attitude, the sculpture recalls to our mind one of the grandest scenes in Hindu mythology. The work is, however, of comparatively recent date, the mantapam having been built in 1770 A. D.

From the Kambattadi Mantapam we pass on to the gate opening out from the inner enclosure. On both sides of the gate, along the aisle running between it and the Kambattadi Mantapam, may be seen four huge figures of Bhairava, Virabhadra, Sabhapathi and Kali, which are various forms of Siva and his divine consort. They are all of full size and monolithic, and show great spirit and freedom of execution. Each figure has an individuality of its own. The first is especially noticeable for its fine proportions, the second for its details, the third for the expression of solemnity on its face, and the fourth for that of fierceness. These figures are situated in a dark recess and are not therefore much noticed by the casual visitor. But they are some of the finest specimens of South Indian sculpture and will bear comparison with any of the best productions of Gandhara or ancient Greece. We may call the attention of the curious tourist to a small, quaint, mournful figure of an old woman at the base of one of these huge figures. She is generally shown to the visitor as Kanchenamala, the old mother or nurse of Minakshi, sorrowing that her beautiful daughter had been given in marriage to a mendicant (as Siva delighted to show himself

Interior of the Thousand Pillars' Mantapam of the Temple, Madura.

From a Photo by J. W. H. Joshua, Madura.

sometimes). Her grief is very well depicted on her face.

Now we may pass out through the gate into the Viravasanta Mantapam, said to have been built by Muthu Virappa Naik (1609-1623) the predecessor of Tirumala. Here also is a Tiruvachi, the arch of lamps, like the one at the entrance to Minakshi's shrine. In front is Nandi, the sacred bull, guarding the gateways to his Lord's abode. On the left is the famous Hall of 1000 columns. Of this monument, Fergusson, the great authority on Indian architecture, says: "Their (of the pillars) sculpture surpasses those of any other Hall of its class I am acquainted with. There is a small shrine dedicated to the goddess Minakshi (this is a mistake for Sabhapathi), the tutelary deity of the place, which occupies the space of 15 columns, so that the real number is only 985. But it is not the number, but the marvellous elaboration, that makes the wonder of the place and renders it in some respects more remarkable than the Choultrie (the Pudumantapam) about which so much has been said and written. I do not feel sure that this Hall

The Hall of 1000 columns.

alone is not a greater work than the Choultrie taken in conjunction with the other buildings of the temple. It certainly forms a far more imposing group." We are sorry that, while Fergusson was no doubt deeply impressed with the grandeur of the monument, and while he clearly understood that the wonder of the place did not consist in the mere number of its pillars, he has not pointed out in greater detail what the elaboration that he admires consists in, or what exactly is the element of beauty or grandeur in the Hall that excites our admiration. As a result of his omission, certain writers, with the false pretence of following him, have likewise in general terms praised its grandeur, but in their utter ignorance of the elementary canons of art criticism have betrayed their singular incapacity to understand the true merits of its construction and have fallen into those very errors against which the great writer took pains to warn his readers. They admire the prodigious number of its pillars or the sculpture on individual columns; and some others again with greater honesty of conviction condemn it as a mere architectural jumble without any appreciable design, and make it an occasion to expostulate upon the peculiar want of a sense of public utility manifested by our ancestors in their architectural undertakings. Before attempting an explanation, it may be mentioned that the Hall of Thousand Columns at Madura is *not the only specimen* of its kind. It is to be seen in many other South Indian temples. It is infact a prominent feature of the Dravidian style of religious architecture. The real wonder of the monument appears to us to be this:—At any position inside the Hall, in consequence of the peculiar arrangement of the pillars, there open up around us sixteen colonnades of varying width and of such length on each side that the perspective afforded by them is simply marvellous; it arrests the attention, overpowers the imagination and draws forth unconscious applause. This is the magic of the place. Instead of being lost in a forest of pillars that obstruct our view and obsess us at every turn, we find that, on the other hand, at every step we take, the pillars re-arrange themselves with kaleidoscopic effect; new colonnades open up and our view is enabled to reach the outer light through a converging perspective of stone columns. As such the Hall must be considered to be an architectural wonder indeed. In order to secure this wonderful effect the architect must have laboured to make all the pillars of exactly the same size and shape and to place them in mathematically accurate positions. The slightest deviation from this symmetry of shape, size and position in any single column out of the 985 would have caused it either to protrude or to recede and would have spoilt the regular formation of the colonnade of which it is a member and would have ultimately marred the effect of the whole. Then again the construction had to satisfy the further conditions of a given number of pillars. It had to form a perfect square and rise in a gallery of three stages.

Then, coming to details, the figures attached to the pillars are carved out of marble-like black granite capable of taking the finest polish. They are all of them of very rare beauty and are models of charm, elegance and taste and have been considered unequalled by any found elsewhere in Southern India. What makes them such worthy objects of admiration is perhaps the freedom from convention and the consequent boldness of execution exhibited in them. Unhappily some of them

The Thousand Pillars' Mantapam ; inside the Temple, Madura.

From a Photo by J. W. H. Joshua, Madura.

have had to bear the brunt of barbarous attacks and have lost a limb or two ; but in spite of mutilation they retain their charm. There are various other minor points of beauty worthy of observation.

The Hall served in a most satisfactory manner the purpose for which it was intended, namely the worship of the deity by a large crowd of people at one and the same time. With the materials given, namely stones, and the use of timber and bricks forbidden, it is extremely doubtful if any other kind of structure could have been planned and built that would at the same time have accommodated so large a gathering and afforded scope for all of them to have a sight of the central deity. It appears to us that the ancient architect has in this single monument of his achievements justified his title to undying fame and vindicated himself from the charges so commonly brought against him by some critics that he lacked a sense of unity and aim and being partial to details he lost sight of the effect of the whole.

At the entrance to the Hall is a mutilated equestrian statue of Ariyanayaka, the famous

Minister of Visvanatha Naik and the father of the Poligar system of Southern India. Tradition ascribes the building of the Hall to the munificence of Ariyanayaka, and as such it is one of the oldest parts of the temple.

The Kalyana Mantapam.

There is one other beautiful spot which remains to be described, and it is the Kalyana Mantapam. It is situated on the way leading from the Hall of 1000 columns to Minakshi Naik's mantapam. It is the only wooden structure in the temple and is modern (having been built in 1707, according to Ferguson (?)). Its roof is covered by copper plates in the form of tiles. In the month of April, the God's marriage is celebrated in the Hall, when it is most elaborately decorated. The Hall is long and spacious and is occasionally used for holding religious and public meetings. In one corner of the mantapam is a quaint little figure of Gundodara, the pot-bellied attendant of Siva. The Sacred Chronicle gives the following account of this imp. When the marriage celebrations were over, a large quantity of food stuffs gathered for the occasion remained unspent. Minakshi, half in pride and half in jest, mentioned the fact to her husband, hinting thereby at the smallness of his following. Siva retorted that he had left his attendants behind for fear of short supplies at Madura and remarked that he would be thankful if even one single man from among the younger members of his retinue could be fed to satisfaction. At the same time he made the all-consuming fire that manifests itself at the end of the world to enter the stomach of his follower Gundodara, who was thereupon seized with a voracious appetite and therefore ate up in a very short time all the rice that had been cooked, and asked for more. The stores were then thrown open, only to be emptied in an instant. And when at last nothing was left to eat he called for drink and exhausted all resources, not excluding the tanks in the city. Having thus made havoc of all that was available in the form of food and drink the insatiable Gundodara went into the presence of Sundaresa and complained to him in the hearing of Minakshi, and to her great chagrin, that he had been starved, and most piteously begged for a handful of water. Siva put his hand immediately on the earth and then and there began the river Vaigai to flow by.

The space between Kalyana Mantapam and the Minakshi Naik's mantapam is occupied by small shops where jewels, bangles and trinkets of all description are sold to the great delight of the children and the girls who scarcely fail to go round the temple every evening.

We have now made a complete circuit of the temple and shall leave it by the tower in front of the God's shrine.

The Pudu Mantapam.

Stepping across the street we enter the Pudu mantapam or the New Pavilion (new in Tirumala's days); otherwise known as the Vasanta mantapam or, as strangely called by Fergusson, Tirumala's "Choultrie", built by Tirumala at a cost of a million sterling and completed in 22 years. It is a three-aisled, rectangular hall measuring 333 ft. by 105 ft. (according to Fergusson) supported by four rows of columns, all elaborately sculptured. The central columns have attached to them life size figures of the ten Naik kings from Visvanatha, the founder of the city, to Tirumala, whose statue is more finely executed than the rest. The façade of this Hall is adorned with

Western Entrance of the New Choultry, Madura, or Tirumal Naik's Pudu Mantapam.

From a *Photo* by J. W. H. Joshua, Madura.

Yalis, monsters of the lion type, trampling on an elephant, and by groups of warriors sitting on rearing horses whose feet rest on the shields of foot soldiers. It is remarkable that the sculpture here is more of a secular nature. "As works exhibiting difficulties overcome by patient labour they are unrivalled by anything found elsewhere." At the western end of the Hall is a small porch of polished black marble used as a pedestal for the God during the spring festival. The Hall is surrounded by a moat also built of stone. The outer bank of the moat is occupied by shops dealing in metal wares, fancy cotton goods and miscellaneous articles. But for ten days in the month of May or June every year, during the spring festival, the shops are closed, the Hall is beautifully decorated, the moat is filled with water and floating lotuses and the God is brought into the porch every evening and worshipped by the gathering multitudes. The Hall is also occasionally used for municipal elections and public meetings.

The Rayagopuram.

Just in front of the eastern entrance to the Pudu Mantapam are to be seen the solid foundations of an unfinished tower, which, if it had been completed, would probably have been the finest edifice of its class in all Southern India. Even in its incompleteness it silently proclaims the glory and magnificence of both the prince who commenced it, and the prince in whose honour it was to have been constructed. The basement covers an area of 174 ft. by 107 ft., and the entrance is nearly 22 ft. wide. The door posts, consisting of single blocks of granite covered with the most exquisite scroll patterns of elaborate foliage, are 60 feet high. The other carvings display the highest skill and excellence. "Being unfinished and consequently never consecrated, it has escaped whitewash and above all the other buildings in Madura its beauties can still be admired in their original perfection." This unfinished edifice is known as the Rayagopuram in honour of the Rāya or Emperor of Vijayanagar whose feudatories the Naiks of Madura were. It is stated that Tirumala laid the foundations of 47 or 63 other such towers in honour of the Rāya. But which exactly of the Rāyas is the one whose memory these are meant to commemorate is yet a matter of dispute. It may be Krishna Deva Rāya, the greatest by far of all the Vijayanagar Emperors. Or, more probably, it may be his successor, Achyutha Rāya, whose southern expedition must still have been fresh in the minds of the people in the early days of Tirumala's reign. These 47 or 63 gopurams were, however, never completed, not because perhaps they were undertakings beyond the means of the prince, but because of the unhappy quarrels that broke out in the latter years of Tirumala's reign which finally led to his declaration of independence of Vijayanagar supremacy. Whatever the real cause the Rayagopuram stands unfinished to-day and points a moral to mortals passing by.

The Seven Seas.

Not far from the Rayagopuram lies the Elukadal or the Seven Seas. The Sacred Chronicle solemnly records that the tank contains the springs of the Seven Seas and owes its existence to the following miracle of Sundaresvara. Minakshi's putative mother expressed a longing for a sea-bath, the spiritual efficacies of which she had heard extolled in the Puranas. When the wish was communicated to Sundaresvara, out of his divine powers he caused the springs of the Seven Seas to rise within the precincts of Madura. When a further difficulty arose by reason of the widowhood of his mother-in-law which state did not guarantee the entire result of the bath, he was so gracious as to restore her husband to life. And when the happy pair came out of their bath in the purificatory waters of the Seven Seas, the heavens opened and a celestial car appeared and bore them away to the abode of the Gods. The tank has, however, fallen on unhappy days now and remains neglected and filled with moss and weeds.

FESTIVALS.

Puja is prescribed to be performed five times in the day, at 5 a.m., 8 a.m., 12 noon, 6 p.m. and 12 midnight. But the Bhattars (priests) are permitted to make puja at any time of the day at the request of visitors. Of course the Bhattar has to be propitiated along with the deity.

Festivals are held on ten prescribed days every month besides many more on other days. The more important of them take place in the months of Chitrai, Avani, Purattasi and Tai.

The Chitrai Festival.—In the bright half of the month of Chitrai (April—May) occurs the

A Car Procession, Madura.

From a Photo by J. W. H. Joshua, Madura.

most important festival, when thousands of people visit Madura from very distant parts of Southern India. It is the month of the marriage of Sundaresvara and Minakshi and the festival celebrates this occasion. This is the best season to visit the place. During this period the town is decorated and presents a gay appearance. The marriage takes place in the Kalyana Mantapam already described. The day after the marriage the Gods are set in two huge and beautiful chariots, said to have been presented to the temple by the Rajah of Ramnad, and the chariots are dragged in procession through the four Masi streets. A large number of people are fed in the temple on the occasion. On the day following, the festival shifts to the bed of the Vaigai river. The scene changes. Sundaresvara and Minakshi are left behind in the city in conjugal felicity and people congregate in the bed of the river early in the morning to welcome Alagar, the God of Alagar Koil, a place 18 miles to the north-east of Madura. For miles together one may see large crowds of people. The story says that Alagar was the brother of Minakshi and was coming to attend his sister's wedding. But when he arrived on the outskirts of

Madura he heard that the marriage had taken place. He was greatly disappointed, and, feeling the slight, resolved to return without even crossing the river and stepping into the town. Even now all the formalities and courtesy are kept up, but the God returns after touching the river. For a considerable length the bed of the river is occupied during the festival by pandals, shops, and shows of all sorts. The common vow to Alagar is a clean shave, and all children and many grown up men and women of the lower castes are shaved bald that morning. Alagar moves down the river leisurely during a period of three days, which are occasions of the greatest rejoicing to the people. The occasion is also utilized for holding a large cattle fair where bulls from different parts of the country are brought and sold. In recent years, the Madura District Agricultural and IndustrialAssociation has attempted to strengthen and organise the cattle fair. The festival brings into the Alagarkoil Treasury an annual income of about Rs. 10,000, in the way of cash and jewels put by pilgrims into the undial (offering) boxes following the God in carts. The most conspicuous and beautiful thing to see in the river bed on the occasion is the picturesquely decorated chapra or improvised chariot of Alagar.

The Puttu Festival.—In the month of Avani again there is a great festival in the river, but this time higher up in its course. The Gods are taken to the river and remain there for a day. The exploits and miracles performed by the Gods at Madura in olden days are enacted here by the temple priests. The allusion is briefly this: The great Saivite Saint and Poet, Manikkavachagar, while he was Prime Minister of the Pandya King, was commissioned to go to a distant country and purchase horses for the King's cavalry. But the Minister was such a great devotee of Siva that piety got the better of duty in him and he spent all the money in building temples for Siva. When finally he made his appearance at Madura he was arrested and put in prison by the king for misappropriation of public funds. But the next morning a troop of horses, finely caparisoned and commanded by a general, appeared before the palace gates and announced their arrival as at the instance of the Minister's orders. The King was immensely pleased and set the Minister at liberty, and the Minister wondered.

For really the commander was Siva himself in disguise and the stud of horses but wild jackals so transformed. When they remained in the stables for a few days they could not eat grass and being starved broke loose, attacked the real horses, killed the grooms and fled away in confusion to the woods. The King took the Minister to task whom he accused of vile trickery and put him to torture. This treatment of a pious and well-intentioned devotee provoked the wrath of the Deity who sent a fierce flood down the river Vaigai. Everything was in danger. The city itself was about to be swept away by the wild torrent. At this juncture, the King called together a Council and determined to allot the task of raising an embankment to every householder in the city. An old, helpless, poor woman, a confectioner by profession, could find no one to do her portion of the King's command. While she was thus in distress Siva himself appeared as a common day labourer and bargained to carry out her wish in exchange for a few sweet cakes that she baked. But instead of busying himself about his duty he loitered about and got cake after cake as they came out of the pan, and finally retired to the shade of a tree to take a

Gods of the Kochadai Iyyanar Temple, Madura.

From a Photo by J. W. H. Joshua, Madura.

midday nap. The King came round to inspect the progress of the work and was all wrath at the negligence of the old woman, who in her turn pointed to the labourer. The King took his whip and laid it sharply on the back of the slumbering cooly, who woke up and with but a shovel of mud thrown against the rushing torrent miraculously stopped its current and disappeared instantaneously to the amazement of the beholders. At the same time the sharp cut of the whip on the back of the divine cooly was felt on the backs of all human beings, not excluding the King, and left its mark there. Now the King could see that it was the work of God himself and he implored him for forgiveness. He was himself asked in turn to forgive his Minister. From this incident the festival derives its name of the "festival of puttu or confection." It would appear that this festival is as old as the days of the early Pandyas.

The Navaratri.—In the month of October during the Dasara festival, the Goddess sits in state and is considered to be very fierce and powerful. Special pujas and incantations are offered. Hundreds of Hindus, women particularly, resort to the temple and remain there sometimes for days and nights together praying for special favours, such as the birth of a child, the return of a runaway husband or the exorcism of evil spirits.

The Teppam Festival—Another very important festival comes round in the month of January, when the Gods are taken to the big tank to the east of Madura and placed in a beautifully decked float, improvised for the occasion, and dragged round three times. As the celebrations take place at night the tank is beautifully illuminated with myriads of little lamps twinkling all about. The sight is unique and impressive. A display of fire-works brings the festivities to a close. It is said that the tank was built by Tirumala Naik and the festival celebrates his birthday.

Temple management.—The management of the temple and its property is vested in a Devasthanam Committee consisting of 5 members elected for life. Under the Committee is a paid manager in immediate executive charge. The temple is one of the richest in Southern India. Its income is derived from

Tasdik allowances, the rents of villages belonging to the temple, rents of shops, stalls, mantapams and other buildings and sites in different parts of the town and from the collections in the Hundi boxes. The annual income on the whole amounts to about Rs. 90,000. Occasional grants and donations add to the temple chest. The Nattukkottai Chetties particularly have done much for the good repair and proper upkeep of the temple.

We have described the temple very briefly. Considerations of space have necessitated the omission of a number of minor deities and secluded portions of the temple. The pavilion of Tirugnana Sambandhar, the great Tamil saint, the smaller Hall of 1000 Pillars, Javandisvarar's shrine, the great bell whose sweet ring is heard from the most distant outskirts of the city, the southern tower, the most pitcuresque of the towers, have had to be left unnoticed. The temple jewels, vahanams and cars are worth seeing as very good specimens of the finest art of the country. Many an interesting exploit of Siva has also had to be omitted. Interested readers are referred for more detailed accounts to the Sthalapuranam, the Sacred Chronicle of Madura.

Again, any historical account of the temple buildings must in the present state of our knowledge be meagre and unsatisfactory. The temple records still remain unexplored and the inscriptions in the inner parts of the temple unread. Judging from our present knowledge it would seem that the general plan was laid down by Visvanatha Naik and the construction of the central shrines and the outermost walls and towers was commenced during his reign. In the succeeding generations, princes, nobles and wealthy devotees completed the remaining portions piecemeal, of course without deviating from the original plan. Experts are of opinon that the temple cost Rs. 11,905,000 and took 120 years for its completion.

The "forced labour" theory.

The history and description of the temple briefly outlined in the preceding paragraphs must be sufficient to deal a deathblow to the current "forced labour" theory of the construction of the large architectural undertakings of our country in ancient times. How grossly false is the statement so commonly made by a certain class of critics that our huge temples were built by powerful kings and emperors by forced labour must be apparent from what has been said before. When they make the assertion, these critics have in mind or suggest to others a state of affairs similar to that prevailing in the old Roman provinces, where rich landlords owned colonies of slaves working under them, or perhaps to that of the old Persian army, where the soldier had to be driven to battle at the sharp point of the whip. They have been led into such false reasonings by their ignorance of local and particular history. It has now been clearly established that such a system of slavery did not prevail in India in ancient or at any rate in mediæval times; that our huge South Indian temples were not built by any such means of forced labour is amply borne out by the history of their growth. To take the Madura temple as an instance we find that the general plan was laid down and the most prominent parts were constructed by Visvanatha Naik, but the remaining portions—they were even larger than that undertaken by that prince—were left to private and individual munificence. The Hall of 1000 Pillars, the Minakshi Naik's Mantapam, the Kambattadi Mantapam, the Mudali Mantapam and a lot of others were built at their own cost by persons whose names they bear. There is absolutely no evidence to show that these persons owned gangs of slaves like the Roman landowners, nor had they either the authority or the real power to compel "forced labour." Serfs attached to the soil were certainly not available for such non-agricultural purposes in towns: The labourers perhaps received low wages and were even paid only in kind without the intervention of money. But such labour cannot be construed as "forced labour." We hope that when the history of the other South Indian temples also comes to be written and is carefully looked into they will give the lie direct to the "forced labour" theory which has been pressed into service by some for purposes of political controversy.

The Perumal Kovil and other Temples at Madura.

The Perumal Kovil.

Besides the temple of Minakshi which is situated in the centre of the city there are a few others of minor importance. As they possess some architectural and antiquarian value, we

Goddess Kali and God Karupanasamy, Madura.

From a Photo by J. W. H. Joshua, Madura.

will describe one or two of them. The chief of these is the Perumal Kovil, situated in the south-western part of the city. The temple is really an old one though portions have been renewed, and can claim as great an antiquity, if not greater, as the town itself or its premier temple of Minakshi. There are references to this temple in the Madura Sthalapuranam. The priests declare that the temple has a mahātmyam or chronicle of its own, which is not, however, available in print. The temple is undergoing repair and renewal. One of the inner shrines has been completely rebuilt. The really old parts of the temple still remaining intact are: one of the inner shrines, the outermost walls, and two small porches built of polished black granite. It appears to have been patronised by the Naik kings who were Vaishnavites, but, after them, it fell into ruin and became the hiding place of dacoits and other undesirables.

Its architecture.

The architecture of the temple, in spite of modern innovations, deserves study on account of the light that it throws on the growth and development of the ancient Dravidian architecture. It may be noted that though the modern architects employed for the renewal of the temple have made attempts at improvements according to their own lights, they have fortunately stuck to the old pattern and have retained its main features. Further, what is left of the old structure is sufficient to give us an idea of the old edifice that has just disappeared. If the structure of the temples of Southern India be studied, the Dravidian type of architecture may be said to subdivide itself into two slightly different styles. Madura supplies specimens of both these styles. The architecture of the Minakshi temple belongs to one class and has already been described. The Perumal temple illustrates the second class. The famous Tanjore temple may also be said to belong to this class. We may note some of the leading features of plan and structure of the second style which go to differentiate it from the first. Simplicity, unity, and elegance are the keynotes of this style. The Hall of 1000 Pillars, that is so prominent in the temples of the other class, is here conspicuous by its absence. Miscellaneous pavilions, cloisters, mantapams and turrets have been excluded with puritanic taste. Unity and proportion of the parts to the whole have been attained by strictly confining the structure to the essential needs of worship. The chief tower stands in the centre of the temple and rises from a square basement in a perfectly pyramidal shape. It is capped by a circular cupola and ends in a pointed golden sikharam or top. The other towers of the temple are subordinated to this central one and help to heighten its effect. The towers in the other style, those found in the Madura, Srirangam and Chidambaram temples, rise from an oblong basement, are indented all round by a number of bays and taper in a graceful curve towards the top. They end in a cylindrical form lying along the top horizontally, and are ornamented by 7, 9 or 12 sikharams as space permits. As regards the arrangement of the towers with reference to one another, this style exactly reverses the order obtaining in the other. It puts the tallest towers outermost, the shortest in the centre and others between in a descending order of magnitude. Both the styles satisfy the highest aims of art. The one appeals directly to our tastes and feelings with its simplicity, its apparent unity and its elegance resulting from freedom from detail and singleness of structure ; the other puzzles our intellect and excites our wonder with its elaboration, its diversity of detail and its huge proportions. It demands a studied appreciation. A reference to the dates shows that the simpler style preceded the more complex and elaborate in accordance with the normal laws of historical development.

The presiding deity of the Perumal Kovil is called Kudal Alagar, or the Alagar of Kudal, the old name for Madura, a name full of historic associations. In the lowest story of the central tower, the God is enthroned in a sitting posture; in the second story in a reclining attitude and in the third and highest, he is standing, drawn up to his full height. The windows of the shrine are beautifully decorated with lattice work in stone. The temple has a tank for the teppam festival.

The Nanmaitharuvar and other temples.

The temple dedicated to Siva in the form of Nanmaitharuvar—the Bestower of Benefits—is situated close by. The Sthalapuranam says in regard to this temple, that Madura was once threatened with floods, the God

Front entrance of the Palace, Madura.

From a Photo by J. W. H. Joshua, Madura.

saved the city and had a temple built by the king. The temple of Rajagopalaswami is also in the neighbourhood. The temple of Tiruvappadayar is situated beyond the Vaigai.

The Tirumal Naik's Mahal and other Buildings.

The remains of the secular architectural structures of the Naik kings at Madura are many and lie over the whole of the south-eastern portion of the modern town. In the 16th and 17th centuries, when the town faced eastwards, the whole of the front half of the fort seems to have been occupied by palaces, mansions, pavilions, elephant stables, barracks and so forth. The western extensions of the town have taken place since the opening of the railway, which has practically turned the general course of town traffic westwards, so that now we may be said to enter the town by the back entrance. Of the architectural remains most have passed into private hands and have been so modified by additions and alterations effected for purposes of dwelling that they cannot be recognised from outside. But when once inside such houses, we are brought face to face with the massive walls, the arched ceiling, the huge pillars, sometimes a small dome here, a vaulted porch there, dark and narrow corridors resounding to the tread of foot-steps—unmistakably the remains of perhaps the royal elephant stables or the residence of some noble lord. They are still in a strong and substantial condition. To pull down some of these massive buildings of the old times has cost in some cases as much labour as to build new ones.

The Palace.

Of those that still remain in the hands of the Government only two or three are in any degree entire and deserve our attention. All of them have been brought under the Act for the Preservation of Ancient Monuments. The style of architecture employed in these is entirely different from that of the temple, and the points of difference will be noticed later. The block of buildings lying in the south-eastern part of the town is generally what is known as the Tirumal Naik's Mahal or Palace. What is now left must be only a small part of the extensive palace buildings of Tirumala and his predecessors. There are extensive ruins just round the palace now converted into the houses of private individuals. Large heaps and mounds were until recently the quarries for brick and stone for house builders in that part of the city. It is not uncommon that while digging for wells old foundations have had to be cleared or the digging given up as impossible. Cellars and underground passages have been met with and covered up while digging for foundations. It would cause no surprise if we remember that when Chokkanatha, the grandson of Tirumala, shifted his residence to Trichinopoly and conceived the idea of erecting a new palace there, he pulled down the palace at Madura for the polished granite pillars, lintels and other valuable materials of building that it contained. A friendly hand guided by a wanton spirit of vandalism worked greater destruction to the beautiful edifices than even the fire and sword of an avowed enemy. We have no idea as to the exact nature of the buildings thus pulled down—whether they were more or less valuable than those which survive.

The existing block consists of two oblong halls, one leading into the other. No description, however graphic, can convey an adequate idea of the artistic design, the fine proportions, and the majestic grandeur of this lofty and massive edifice. What can be attempted here must be more of the nature of general remarks than any detailed description. The proportion of the parts to the whole is so correct, every part has been so worked up with the view of enhancing the beauty of the whole, that from outside the palace makes but a poor impression, but when once we are in the court-yard what looked to be a small building from a distance appears to expand and assume its true proportions—so new, so lofty, so huge and yet so elegant, that we are agreeably surprised and more than satisfied. Fergusson gives some details: "The principal apartments in the palace at Madura are situated round a court-yard which measures 244 by 142 ft. surrounded by arcades of very great beauty. The pillars which support the arches are of stone, 40 ft. in height, and are joined by foliated brick arcades of great elegance of design. The whole of the ornamentation is worked out in the exquisitely fine stucco called chunam or shell-lime which is a characteristic of the Madras Presidency. On one side of the Court stands the Swarga Vilasam or celestial pavilion, for-

Pillars, Northern side, inside the Palace, Madura.

From a Photo by J. W. H. Joshua, Madura.

merly the throne room of the palace (now used by the District Court of Madura). It is an arcaded octagon covered by a dome 60 ft. in diameter and 70 ft. in height. On another side of this Court is placed another splendid hall. This one in its glory must have been as fine as any. The Hall itself is said to be 120 ft. by 67 ft. and its height to the centre of the roof is 70 ft. But what is more important than its dimensions is that it possesses all the structural propriety of a Gothic building. It is evident that if the Hindus had persevered a little longer in this direction they would have accomplished something that would have surpassed the works of their masters in this form of art."

The beauty of the palace is now marred by screens, tattees, and wooden obstructions set for dividing it into compartments for the use of the public offices. It is now kept in good repair, but in the eighties it had been left uncared for. Lord Napier, Governor of Madras, to whose refined taste the new buildings in Madras and elsewhere owe their style and beauty, drew the attention of the Government to its neglected state, and in a strong minute insisted upon its preservation. Since then a large sum of money has been spent on its upkeep and it is now preserved under the Act passed by Lord Curzon for the preservation of the ancient monuments of the land.

As regards the style of architecture it will be noticed that it is entirely different from the one adopted in the temple and the Pudumantapam, which last was erected by the same monarch and at the same time as the palace. The material used in the temple is solely stone ; in the palace it is stone and brick. In both timber has been eschewed. While in the temple the horizontal roofing is the rule without exception, the dome and the arch predominate in the secular edifice. Indeed the principle of the arch has been made use of in the palace and the other large buildings of its class for almost any and every purpose. The gateway, the dome, the vaulted porch, the corridors, all embody the same principle. It cannot, however, be said that it has been carried to a fault. The strength of these old structures is due largely to this method of construction in which the utmost strength is imparted to the bricks by subjecting them to opposing sets of

Southern Row of Pillars, The Palace, Madura.

From a Photo by J. W. H. Joshua, Madura.

lateral pressures. Considering the trying effects of our climate it is wonderful that these built with such material have resisted the destructive forces of nature for such a long time.

Fergusson states that the use of the arch and the dome was learnt by the Hindus of Vijayanagar from the Mahomedans of the neighbouring kingdom of Bijapur. But it is admirable that with rare sagacity they borrowed only the strong points of the Saracenic art leaving out the weak ones, and what is more they completely adapted what they borrowed to suit their own needs. For instance the minaret is not to be found in the Hindu monuments. The dome and the arch were selected. The chief points about the dome are its great strength, its elegance and sometimes its acoustic properties; it also covers a large space without the intervention of pillars. For the details of ornamentation the architects fell back upon their own resources.

Now the Naiks of Madura had been originally sent out from Vijayanagar and were for a long time the feudatories of the Empire. In most matters they closely followed the example and reproduced the institutions of Vijayanagar. In the organisation of the army, in the collection of revenue, in the patronage of temples, in the establishment of choultries, in State etiquette and paraphernalia and many other matters both public and private, the monarchs of Madura imitated their imperial masters. The civilizing influence thus exerted by the Vijayanagar Empire over the whole of Southern India was immense and has survived to our own days in the courts of the Native States. It is therefore not surprising that the Mahal resembles some old Vijayanagar buildings. The Tamkum Pavilion is identical in name, plan and structure with the garden pavilion at Vijayanagar (an illustration of which may be found in the pages of Fergusson or Sewell's 'Forgotten Empire").

The Tamkum Bungalow.

The Tamkum Pavilion, now converted into a bungalow, is situated close to the Dufferin Park on the northern bank of the Vaigai. It is another beautiful little architectural relic of the same style as the Palace. Oral tradition assigns the building of it to Tirumala, but the tablet put up by the Government on its preser-

View inside the Palace, Madura.

vation under the Ancient Monuments Preservation Act speaks of it as having been built by Mangammal in 1730. It may have been intended as a garden pavilion, as the term itself means in Telugu—as a summer house to which the princes could resort from the oppressive heat of the day. Over a square basement of stone, about 15 ft. high, stands a hall covered by a masonry dome 21½ ft. across, in the shape of an inverted lotus, supported at the tips of the petals by walls radiating from and forming an outer veranda to the hall. The central hall is completely protected from the heat of the sun but at the same time so open on all sides as to afford a full view of the surrounding landscape and ample ventilation. The arches are crenulated and are exceedingly beautiful. It is a pity that in the recent additions made to the edifice, the same style was not adopted. The District Collector resides in the bungalow, and the rent collected goes towards the maintenance of a scholarship known as the Tamkum Scholarship.

The Collector's office, and the Taluk office are also old buildings of the Naik style and times. The latter is credited with having been the palace of Mangammal. It was used for a long time as the district jail.

The Teppa-kulam.

The Teppakulam, known commonly as the Vandiyur or Mariamman Teppakulam, is situated about 2 miles to the south-east of Madura. It is an artificial reservoir built by Tirumal Naik for the use of Minakshi. It is almost a square, measuring 1,000 ft., by 950 ft., and curiously enough occupies the same area as the Minakshi temple. It may be stated that it is the largest stone-built tank in the whole of Southern India. "The sides are faced all round with cut granite and surmounted by a handsome parapet of the same material, just inside which a granite paved walk, five feet wide, runs all round the tank. Flights of steps, three on each side, run down at intervals to the water's edge. In the middle of the reservoir is a square island, also faced with cut granite, on which among green palms and flowering trees is a small white temple with a tower of the usual kind flanked at the four corners of the island with graceful little mantapams." The whole is exceedingly well proportioned and graceful in effect. Tradition points

Big Teppa-Tank, with boundary wall, Western side, Madura.

From a Photo by J. W. H. Joshua, Madura.

The Teppa Tank, Madura.

From a Photo by J. W. H. Joshua, Madura.

to the spot as the place from which the bricks for Tirumala's palace were made and says that when the clay was being dug out, the big stone image of Ganapathi now in the temple was found buried under the ground. At this auspicious find the king converted the excavations into this beautiful tank. It is used once in the year for the Teppam festival described elsewhere.

CHAPTER III.

THE MADURA MUNICIPALITY.

The Madura Municipality is the largest moffussil municipality in the Presidency. In accordance with the old Town Improvement Act of 1865 the town of Madura was constituted a municipality on the 1st of November 1866. The Council originally consisted of 16 members, of whom 7 were elected and the rest nominated by Government. At various times, afterwards, the number was increased until it reached the present figure of 25, of whom 18 are elected. The Council is now presided over by a full timed paid Chairman on a salary of Rs. 400—600.

"The permanent visible improvements" says the District Gazetteer "effected by this body since it was first established are many. In 1871-1872 a municipal office was provided by altering at a cost of Rs. 5,000 an outlying building belonging to Tirumal Naik's palace. In the same year was put up the clock which adorns one of the two turrets at the east end of the palace. In 1873 the then Maternity Hospital was extended at a cost of Rs. 25,000, and in July 1876, the branch dispensary on which Rs. 18,000 had been spent was opened. In 1884 the causeway across the Vaigai was put in thorough repair, trees were planted in the streets, the People's Park, otherwise known as the Dufferin Park, was formed and the first water-supply project was carried into effect and about the same time the Council subscribed Rs. 10,000 to the bridge across the Vaigai which was opened in 1889 (at a cost of Rs. 2,75,000). The latest notable undertakings have been the opening of the Dispensary for Women and Children in 1894, the laying out of the garden called the Edward Park which was opened on the day of the Coronation of His late Majesty King Edward VII, and the provision of the greater part of the cost of the erection of the excellent new range of buildings for the hospital." Since then a new market has been built to the north-east of the temple and butcher stalls on the western border of the town.

Municipal problems.—Among the many problems that have already cost and are still costing a great deal of money and trouble to the municipality, the foremost are those connected with drainage and water-supply. Various schemes for providing the town with a proper system of drainage have so far proved either too costly or have failed. The chief difficulty met with in this matter is that the central part of the town—being the oldest part—is on a lower level than the surrounding parts. During rains, water collects in the centre of the town and does not find an easy and natural outlet from the town. The rain water collecting within the temple walls falls into the Golden Lily Tank and through an underground passage finds its way to the Yelukadal. The pipe water, which is sufficient for profuse use by the townspeople, and afterwards to fill the street gutters to the intensification of stench and filth, is found insufficient for the introduction of the flushing sytem of drainage.

The other problem of municipal administration—the problem of water-supply—may be said to have been solved to a certain extent, though in the hot weather scarcity is felt. The first water-supply scheme for Madura was to lead a channel from the Vaigai at about 4 miles up the river along an earthern embankment and to fill certain reservoirs in the town. The scheme proved a failure. The crumbling remains of this ingenious project may still be seen on the western outskirts of the town and is attributed by the ignorant to Naikan engineering, which was certainly of a better quality. A new scheme was attempted in 1884 to pump water from wells in the bed of the river near the Mayya Mantapam and to fill up the two large iron cisterns near the Elephant Gate and the Blackburn lantern stand. Still the supply was inadequate to meet the demand. So finally in 1894, the present water-works were constructed and water is now pumped from wells sunk on one bank of the river. The springs frequently fail owing to an underground natural channel which diverts the subsoil current from the river a little to the north of the water-works. So there seems to be a proposal on foot now to construct a trench in the bed of the river to facilitate the flow of the under current in the proper direction.

A few more green enclosures in the heart of the town, a large park with a zoo and recreation grounds, a decent Town Hall, a few institutions of general educative value, like the museum, and a well-equipped public library and reading room, are among the desiderata to make Madura worthy of its great historic past.

Palias, or Jungle people, Madura Hills.

From a Photo by J. W. H. Joshua, Madura.

CHAPTER IV.

THE PEOPLES OF MADURA.

The City of Madura is the second largest in the Presidency in point of population. According to the Census of 1901, the people numbered 105,984—3,750 of them being Christians, 9,120 Mahomedans and the rest Hindus. The population doubled itself during the preceding 30 years and of the various causes which made for this increase, the most important was the completion of the Periyar Project which, while enriching the people in almost all parts of the district, vastly improved the commercial, industrial and economic position of the capital. The opening of the railway line to Ramesvaram has given additional importance to the city as a halfway house to that sacred place of pilgrimage. The town has already expanded beyond its natural limits. On the western side a new colony has sprung up beyond the railway line and on the northern side a far more promising suburb is rising on the northern bank of the river. The Patnulis have pushed their settlement to the end of the road leading to the Teppakulam on the south-eastern side. And causes are still in operation that are full of possibilities for the further expansion of the city in the near future. The opening of the direct communication with Ceylon and the enlargement of the natural harbour at Pamban will undoubtedly divert into this line a large portion of the traffic now passing via Tuticorin and this is bound to make Madura the commercial emporium of the south by reason of her situation. The location of the new Ramnad District offices in Madura will also contribute its quota of official importance to the city.

Madura has already become the home of almost every Indian nationality. Walking along the street we come across men from all parts of India—the plump round-bellied Bengali Babu, the tall and stalwart Punjabi Lala and the busy Bombay Sait. The indigenous population represents all castes and races. The Patnulkarans are strong in numbers. The Nattukottais have in their hands the banking and the speculative concerns of the place. The Kallans form the bulk of the labouring classes. Of the other castes there is not much to be said. The Brahmins still form a strong majority and live round the temple. Forming the brains of the country, they pursue the learned professions. The Mahomedans occupy the south-western part of the town. Some of them are merchants. The local lace-making industry is in their hands. The Christians cluster round the east and west gates. They are mostly Roman Catholics and followers of the American Protestant and the Evangelical Lutheran Missions. We shall now dwell at some length on some of the more important castes in the town.

The Sourashtras.

First of all, the Sourashtras—better known as Patnulkarans—(literally, silk weavers) attract our attention by reason of their numbers. Every third man you come across in the town is a Sourashtra. It is the Sourashtras who have largely contributed to the present commercial importance of the city. As a recent writer in the *Madras Mail* says, "the proud position of Madura to this day as the second city in the Presidency is mainly if not solely due to her prosperous and industrious community of Sourashtra merchants and silk weavers." The Sourashtra is easily distinguished from members of other castes by his yellow complexion, his foreign accent and his shy and awkward manners. He is thin, tall and generally handsome, though showing signs of racial degeneracy. He wears a small tuft on the top of his head, generally puts on namams, wears his dhoti in the Brahmin fashion and carries his sacred thread rather prominently. You would sometimes mistake him for a Brahmin but that his accent is treacherous.

Their origin.

There are several traditions and stories regarding the origin of Patnulkarans or the Sourashtras. They, however, as is always the case in such matters, contain but a very small percentage of truth as their basis.

(i) The story which enjoys the largest currency among the Patnulis themselves is that they were originally Brahmins and lived in Devagiri, supplying the Goddess Lakshmi with a certain amount of silk cloth on the Deepavali day annually; that one particular year their supply fell short and they were in consequence cursed by the Goddess, excommunicated and expelled from the country: that they went in all directions and coming southward one party settled in Tirupathi, Vellore, Tanjore and Madura.

(ii) Another account also largely current among the Patnulis is that they are the descendants of an eponymous Brahmin sage called Tantuvardhana, the improver of threads.

(iii) The true account of their origin, however, is perhaps the one based on an inscription found at Mandāsor or Dasapura in Western Malwa bearing the date 473 A. D. and supported by tradition and ceremonial relics. The inscription narrates in the first instance how a band of Pattavayas or silk-weavers, with their children and kinsmen, came from the district of Lata in Guzerat and settled at Dasapura, and how while some of them took to other professions, the majority devoted themselves to their time-honored profession of silk-weaving and constituted themselves into a separate and flourishing guild. It then proceeds to record that in the reign of Kumaragupta, of the early Gupta dynasty, the flourishing guild of the silk-weavers built a temple to the Sun; that under other kings it fell into disrepair but was again restored by the same guild. The next historical reference that we get of the Pattavayas is from a Marathi manuscript which refers to them as having settled at Devagiri, the modern Doulatabad, then the capital of the Yadavas. It is possible that they emigrated to this place in consequence of impending Mahomedan invasions from the north. Again when Doulatabad was captured and sacked by the mussalmans at the beginning of the 14th century they seem to have sought the protection and patronage of the Emperors of Vijayanagar. When the Naiks began to rule at Madura they induced some of the Pattavayas to come and settle at Madura and supply the court with silk fabrics. In support of this theory of the Sourashtra origin of the Pattavayas or Patnulkarans and of their southern migration various evidences might be quoted. Their language is a corrupt form of Khatri, a dialect of Guzerathi. It has a large admixture of Canarese and Telugu words, borrowed evidently during their passage through the Canarese and Telugu countries. The Patnulis observe the feast of Basavanna which is peculiar to the Deccan country. One of the marriage customs of the community further supports this view of their origin. On the day previous to a Patnuli wedding the members of the bridegroom's party go to the house of the bride and ask formally for the hand of the girl. Her relations ask them in a set form of words who they are, where they come from, and they reply that they are from Sourashtra, they rested a while in Devagiri, travelled farther south to Vijayanagar and thence came on to Madura. They then ask the bride's party the same question in turn and receive the same answer.

Thus the Patnulkarans form a typical example of a caste formed by migration and settlement of one people among another. To whatever caste they belonged in their original homes they have formed in Southern India a separate caste by themselves. In recent years, owing to the increase in numbers and to the subdivision of labour, they have come to be divided still further into sections and subcastes. Among them there is a small priestly class which, however, at present is ignored at Madura. All of them claim to be Brahmins and imitate the ways of the Brahmins in wearing the dhoti and the sacred thread and in other matters; the men generally following the manners of the Iyengar Brahmins and the women those of the Telugu ladies. They put on namams and assume brahminical titles, such as Iyengar, Iyer, Rau, Bhagavathar and Sastrigal. This claim to brahminhood is however disputed, and the remarks of the Madras Census reporter for 1901 are just and must be admitted. "They are" he says "an intelligent and hard-working community and deserve every sympathy in the efforts which they are making to elevate the material prosperity of their numbers and improve their educational condition, but a claim to brahminhood is a difficult matter to establish... * * * In Madura their claim to brahminhood has always been disputed. As early as 1705 A. D. the Brahmins of Madura called in question the Patnulkaran's right to perform 'upakarma' (the renewal of the sacred thread), in the Brahmin fashion. Eighteen members of the community were arrested by the Governor of Madura for performing the ceremony. The matter was taken to the notice of Queen Mangammal and she directed her State pundits to convene a meeting of learned men and to examine into it. On their advice she issued a grant on a palm leaf permitting them to follow the Brahmin rites.

But since all the twice born, whether Brahmins, Kshatriyas or Vaisyas, were entitled to do the same, the grant establishes little."

Customs and manners.

Like the Brahmins, the Sourashtra children are married young. In settling marriages great importance is attached to gotrams. Two favourable planetary situations, one following the other, are necessary in the selection of the muhurtham and as such an auspicious hour is of rare occurrence, a number of marriages take place at the same time—greatly adding to the *eclat* of the occasion and at the same time reducing expenditure. In old days there was a rule that only persons in the same street could intermarry. It is no longer observed. Patnulkara marriage processions in Madura are conspicuous by their length. Even old couples enjoy a repetition of the happy ceremonies on such occasions. Brahminical rites, particularly those of the Telugus, are followed. At the close of every marriage the Rama or Krishna Nataka must be enacted. Widows may not re-marry but are permitted to grow the hair, wear jewels and chew betel.

Though all of them put on namams they are devotees of Vishnu and Siva indiscriminately. The temple of Minakshi is quite a common place of worship for them. Krishna is a favourite deity, to whom they have recently built a temple in their part of the town. They have no special gurus or religious heads but most of them accept the head of the Sringeri Mutt as their spiritual head. Nor have they any special scriptures. Until very recently their language had no written alphabet. One has now been invented and is coming into general use. All of them pass for vegetarians.

Their religion.

As in the Komutti community, a strong *esprit de corps* prevails among the Sourashtras and they are therefore pretty well organised for public purposes. Their communal organisation is the Sourashtra Sabha. It was started in 1895 and it has for its object the management of the affairs of the community as a whole and the safeguarding its interests. A small tax is levied by the association and the collections go to meet the expenses of the educational, religious, and charitable institutions maintained by the community.

Their *esprit de corps.*

Most of the Patnulkarans are engaged in the dyeing and weaving industries. As has already been remarked, they are more cotton weavers than silk weavers now. Some of them are also traders and merchants. Their women help in the easier stages of weaving and also work as day labourers in the town, doing all kinds of sundry work. The community is as a whole a hard-working and industrious class and have attained to high skill in their craft. All the improvements made in the processes of dyeing and weaving in recent times have been due to them.

General remarks.

The Sourashtras in Madura are generally more wealthy, better clothed and better housed than their castemen in other places in Southern India. Though the community must still be said to be a 'backward' class, some of its members have in recent years received higher education and take part in municipal and local administration. One of them recently stood as a candidate for election to the Madras Legislative Council, and the present chairman of the municipality is one of their community.

Like some of the other trading classes, the Patnulis possess a secret trade language. "The most remarkable feature about it," says a well-known Indian writer on ethnographical subjects, "is the number of terms and phrases borrowed from the craft to which special meanings are given. Thus a man of no status is stigmatised as a "rikhta kandu", a spindle without yarn. Similarly a man of little sense is called a 'muddha', the name of a thick peg which holds one side of the roller. Likewise a talkative person is referred to as a 'rhetta'—the roller used for winding the thread upon the spindles which makes a most unpleasant creaking noise. 'Kahmekai' from 'Kahim', a technical term used for cutting the loom off, means to make short work of an undesirable person. A man who is past middle age is called "porkut phillias", which in weavers' parlance means that half the loom is turned".

The Nattukottai Chetties.

The community that next has the greatest interest for the student of Indian Ethnology in Madura is that of the Nattukottai Chetties. The Nattukottai Chetty is easily distinguished from others by his purely Dravidian facial features—

a round face, snub nose, eyes like the petals of a lotus and slightly thick lips and a dull black complexion. He is conspicuous by his clear shaven head besmeared with prominent stripes of sacred ashes, a rudraksham hanging from his neck, the dilated lobes of ears, the gold chain round his loins and the rings on his fingers. They are a rich community and they hold the banking business of the country in their hands. They are highly conservative, exceedingly thrifty, very strict in their monetary transactions and little merciful to their debtors. They have consequently a notoriety for their greed and are naturally not held in good esteem by the members of the other castes who mostly belong to 'the borrowing race of mankind.' They however make up for these defects of character by devout piety and a charitable disposition!

Their origin.

Their stronghold is more in the district than in the town. But all the chief firms are represented in the town. Various accounts of their origin are given—the most agreeable to them being that they belonged to a high caste in Kauveripattanam in old days and migrated from that place to this district owing to severe persecution. Their enemies on the other hand put forth a vile story that they are the bastard descendants of a Mahomedan father and a Kalla mother in proof of which they point to their bald head, dilated lobes of ears and other customs peculiar to the Mussalmans or the Kallans. Etymologically the word Nattukottai is supposed to be derived from Nattarasan Kottai, a village in the Sivaganga Zemindary, where they are said to have first settled. Another account says that in ancient days the Vaisyas of the lunar race were living in the town of Sathiapuri in Naganadu and were a much respected class. Owing to severe persecution in the days of a ruler they migrated and settled at Conjeevaram. Owing to a similar misfortune there also, they quitted the place for Chidambaram. From this latter place they went further South to the Chola Country and finally to Pandi. In the last mentioned country they established three settlements at Ilayathukudi, Sundarapattanam and Ariyur. Thus they became divided into three sections, of which the Ilayathukudi and Sundarapattanam Chetties alone are found at Madura. Not being satisfied with one place of worship they requested the King to give them more temples. Accordingly temples were provided for them at Mathur, Vairavanpatti, Nemam, Iluppankudi, Suvaikudi, and Velankudi. The Nattukottais are at present divided into sub-sections as belonging to one or other of these temple divisions. Only people of the same division intermarry. A similar rule is observed in the adoption of children.

Customs and Manners:—They are still under the patriarchal system of family organisation but it is strongly of a federal type. That is to say, all the members of the family live together in the same house, but the married sons have apartments set apart for them and receive a carefully calculated yearly allotment of rice and other necessaries. This custom has given rise to the building of large houses. A Nattukottai Chetty's house is noted for its large dimensions. When a male child is born, a certain sum of money is usually set apart and in due time the accumulated interest is spent on the boy's education.

Family organisation.

Marriage.

Every Nattukottai Chetty bachelor has to undergo a ceremony preparatory to his marriage. He goes to the temple and after worship he whirls a burning bag of charcoal round his head and then sets fire to a booth constructed for the purpose and marks his forehead with the ashes. Similarly the maid before her marriage replaces the glass beads of maidenhood by gold or silver jewels, going through a set ceremony. After the rites are over she proceeds to her friends' houses to beg for pulses in words similar to these :—"I have come dancing, give me avarakai ; I have come singing, give me padavarangai ; I have come speaking, give me sorakkai." A feast follows in which specially made cakes are distributed among friends and relations.

Every Nattukottai has an inviolable right to the hand of his paternal aunt's daughter. During the marriage, the bridegroom performs the curious ceremony of carrying salt perhaps in memory of a profession once followed by the caste. The tali is tied by an old man who has had a large number of children, assisted by the bridegroom's sister.

The tali is a jewel long and broad and has fork-like projections. Costly talis may be replaced by ordinary ones for everyday use. The marriage contract is generally written out in a palmyra leaf and safely preserved.

Death ceremonies.

Among the death ceremonies the interesting feature is the husking of paddy by the daughters and sisters of the deceased. A pandal or booth is erected in front of the house and must stand for four days. Consequently the word 'pandal' has acquired an odium among them and is scrupulously avoided on auspicious occasions when it is termed a Kottagai.

Some other customs.

As has been said before, the men shave the head completely. "The story goes," explains a writer, "that when the Chola King of Kauveri pattanam persecuted them, the members of the caste resolved not to shave their heads until they quitted his territories. When they reached their new settlement they shaved their heads completely as a memorial of their stern resolution." The members of both the sexes have the lobes of their ears dilated like

Shānars. The women-folk wear necklaces of beads like the Korava women, and take pleasure in making baskets. Disputes between members of the community are always decided by a communal panchayat and public courts of law are avoided as much as possible. Each of the Kovils mentioned above is managed by a Karyakaran who is elected by the elders of the particular temple division. The Karyakaran assisted by a panchayat acts as a court of arbitration for settling disputes. Members refusing to go to arbitration in cases of disputes are refused the garland from the temple on marriage occasions, without which no marriage can take place, and the recalcitrant members are thus kept in wholesome check.

Their occupations and business qualities.

As has been said before, their chief occupation is money-lending; wholesale trade, and other speculative businesses have also in recent years attracted some of them. They scarcely serve any one outside their community. They either trade on their own account or are employed as agents or assistants. It is curious to note that their official year runs on for three consecutive years and it is only at the close of that period that their accounts are audited and closed. The night is considered the best time for business. In Madura their firms are open only at dusk and during the night when all the business transactions are conducted. Though conservative to a degree in their customs and manners, they are excellent men of business. They have freely crossed the 'Kalapani' in pursuit of their trade and carried on their ventures in Ceylon, Burma, Singapore, Eastern Asia, South Africa and Mauritius. Their good faith and honesty are proverbial and have no doubt contributed very largely to their success in all their undertakings. "In organisation co-operation and business methods," writes Edgar Thurston in his "Castes and Tribes of Southern India", "they are as remarkable as the European merchants. Very few of them have yet received any English education. They regard education, as at present given in public schools, as worse than useless for professional men, as it makes them theoretical and scarcely helps in practice. The simple but strict training which they give their boys, the long and tedious apprenticeship, which even the sons of the richest among them have to undergo, make them very efficient in their profession and methodical in whatever they undertake." The training which a Nattukottai boy gets is indeed such as to fit him for his particular profession in life. As a boy he learns accounts, attends the shop of his father and applies himself generally to business. As soon as he marries he has to live separately, though in the same house with his father upon a stringent allotment, every pie spent in excess of which is a special charge on his share of the family property. On the other hand, his savings belong to him exclusively. He has thus every inducement to save rather than to spend. His habits are simple, his living cheap. Everything in his life is calculated to add to his capital. He is thrifty and frugal even to a fault. And many stories are told of his thrift and greed. Even the wealthiest among them lives in the most miserly fashion. His sole aim in life seems to be the making of as much money as possible. His wife assists him by being equally thrifty and by making baskets or spinning thread during her leisure hours. He will unhesitatingly charge his relative with costs if the latter stays in his house longer than a day.

Worldly as they are, they are none the less a very conservative and devout race. They are staunch Saivites by religion, wear a rudraksham in the neck and besmear themselves with sacred ashes. Some of them are strict vegetarians, the rest have no objection to animal food.

Their religion.

They are as charitable as they are religious. In many families a pie in every rupee of profit, and in others a fixed percentage of the profits in business, is always set apart for charity. The funds so collected are utilized in maintaining Sanskrit patasalas or schools for Pundits and Vaidik students who are fed and educated free, and in maintaining choultries and feeding-houses for the poor. A large part of the funds is spent in the renovation and restoration of many of the neglected and forgotten Saivite shrines in this part of the country. The Madura temple owes a great deal to the Nattukottai Chetties for what it is at the present day. In such undertakings preference is shown to those shrines which have been extolled by the Saivite Saints. In justice to them it must be said that the Hindu religion and Hindu temples lie under a great debt of

Their charity.

obligation to them for their patronage and unstinted charity in these days of religious decay and degeneration. Wherever business has taken them, to distant Singapore or far-away Mauritius, they have taken their religion with them and have raised temples to their gods in those foreign lands.

Trade secrets.

Like other trading classes in Southern India, the Nattukottai Chetties have a trade language of their own, which, however, is different in different localities. For instance, the letters of the word Tirupura Sundari stand respectively for 12 As., 8 As., 4 As., 3 As., 2 As., 1, $\frac{3}{4}$ and $\frac{1}{2}$ anna; those of Vadagiri Easvarar Thunai stand respectively for amounts from one to eleven rupees. The table of tens of rupees is made up of the letters of the word Tirukalukundram (the name of a sacred place near Chingleput), the first letter representing ten rupees, the second twenty and so forth.

The Kallans.

Among the peoples of Madura there is another which deserves our attention on account of their primitive customs and ways of life. They are the Kallans—literally the thieves—a caste of people once largely addicted to dacoity and theft, though in recent years they have been tamed to settle down as agriculturists and farm-labourers in the country and as watchmen and menial servants in the town. They are not so easily distinguished from the other Sudras in the streets of Madura. But the student of Indian History may remember them as the "fierce Colliers" described in the pages of "Orme's History." They gave a lot of trouble to the East India Company in the early days of their occupation of Southern India and His Majesty's Government until very recently. They are one of the chief criminal tribes of the south, and statistics go to show that nearly 40 per cent of the convicts in the Madura Jail are Kallans.

General characteristics.

But on the whole they are a brave, fierce and warlike people, fond of independence and freedom of action, though occasionally when the crops fail or they have too much time on their hands, they prove irksome to their neighbours and the Government. They are keen hunters. Their favourite weapon is the

Valaithadi or a curved, short and thick stick, like the boomerang. Their happy days were over with the advent of the policeman and the magistrate under the benign rule of the British; for they can no longer practice with impunity their favourite pursuit of highway robbery or house-breaking. But cattle lifting, which is more profitable and less risky, has taken its place and they are excellent adepts in the art of spiriting cattle away at night. Generally they come at night in a band of three or four, enter the cattle-sheds, remove them, stimulate them with intoxicating liquors and drive them 30 or 40 miles before dawn. They are kept in hiding the whole day and during the next night they are again driven to a great distance so as to be out of all reach of any pursuit. After a week or so they are sold in distant markets. The only successful remedy available to the injured party is to negotiate through a Kallan go-between for the restoration of cattle on payment of a certain sum which generally will not fall short of half their market value. If the 'tuppukuli' or payment for clues, as this blackmail is called, is paid, the cattle will return home or will be

Cattle lifting.

found grazing in the neighbourhood. If, however, the owner of the cattle reports to the police, there is no help for him. The police cannot find them, the Kallan will not restore them afterwards. It must be noted that the Kallan is too shrewd to steal buffaloes as they do not answer his purpose by reason of their slow pace.

Kudikāval.

Another calling which they pursue and which is quite civil and without risk is service as watchmen on a small annual payment. They offer themselves as watchmen to guard your house from theft and dacoity or rather they claim the right to watch and to receive the annual payment called Kudikāval. The refusal to accept their services or pay the blackmail will be followed by the mysterious disappearance of cattle and accidental fires in hayricks. In consideration of a trifling charge made for a real service rendered even the educated think it the better part of prudence to insure themselves with a Kallan against theft and fire.

Their origin.

The original home of the Kallans seems to have been Tondamandalam, or the Pudukkottai country, and the head of the class is to this day called

Tondaman. "They are believed to be a branch of the Kurumbas, who, when they found their regular occupation as soldiers gone, took to marauding and made themselves so obnoxious by their thefts and robberies that the term Kallan or thief was applied and stuck to them as a tribal appellation." They trace their descent to Indra and Ahalya and style themselves 'thevars' like the Maravars. Strange to say, a Kallan is not ashamed of his caste but will boldly say that he belongs to the robber caste and would even defend their national calling by arguments similar to those of Robin Hood of old England.

...

Customs and manners.

The Peramalai Kallars of Madura practise the rite of circumcision. Generally boys of the same age are taken amidst the beating of drums and the blowing of trumpets to a river bank and the customary barber surgeon does the operation. As every Kallan has the right of claiming the hand of his paternal aunt's daughter in marriage, the aunt has to bear the expenses of the ceremony. Similarly the maternal uncle meets the expenses of the ceremony following the puberty of his niece.

Polyandry was common in days gone by but is not now followed. The men wear toe rings. Marital ties are very loose, divorce being quite common. But women are very chaste and true to their affianced. A widow may remarry. By religion they are worshippers of both Vishnu and Siva without any distinction. They are really devotees of village deities, such as Karuppan and Alagar. The famous shrine of Kallar Alagar, 18 miles to the north-east of Madura, is one of their places of pilgrimage. The dead are generally buried. If a woman dies with child, the child is taken out and buried by the side of its mother.

Jellikattu or bull baiting.

A common pastime with the Kallars is the manly game of bull-baiting known as Jellikattu. It is best described in the words of Nelson, the author of "The Madura Country." "This is a game worthy of a bold and free people and it is to be regretted that certain Collectors should have discouraged it under the idea that it is somewhat dangerous. The Jellikattu is conducted in the following manner. On a certain day in the year, large crowds of people, chiefly males, assemble together in the morning in some extensive open space, the dry bed of a river perhaps, or of a tank, and many of them may be seen leading ploughing bullocks, of which the sleek bodies and rather wicked eyes afford clear evidence of the extra diet they have received for some days in anticipation of the great event. The owners of these animals begin to brag of the strength and speed and to challenge all and any to catch and hold them. And in a short time one of the best beasts is selected to open the day's proceedings. A new cloth is made fast round his horns, to be the prize of his captor, and he is then led out into the midst of the arena by his owner and there left to himself surrounded by a throng of shouting and excited strangers. Unaccustomed to this sort of treatment and excited by the gestures of those who have undertaken to catch him, the bullock usually lowers his head at once and charges wildly into the midst of the crowd, who nimbly run off on each side to make way for him. His speed being much greater than that of the men he soon overtakes one of his enemies and makes at him to toss him savagely. Upon this the man drops on the sand like a stone and the bullock instead of goring him, leaps over his body and rushes after another. The second man drops in his turn and is passed like the first; and after repeating this operation several times the beast either succeeds in breaking the ring and galloping off to his village, charging every person he meets on the way, or is at last caught and held by the most vigorous of his pursuers.

"Strange as it may seem the bullocks never by any chance toss or gore anyone who throws himself down on their approach, and danger arises only from their accidentally reaching unseen and unheard someone who remains standing. After the first two or three animals have been let loose one after the other, two or three or even half-a-dozen are let loose at a time; the scene quickly becomes most exciting. The crowd sways violently to and fro in various directions in frantic efforts to escape being knocked over; the air is filled with shouts, screams and laughter, and the bullocks wander over the plain as fiercely as if blood and slaughter were their sole occupation. In this way perhaps two or three hundred animals are run in the course of a day and when all go home in the evening a few cuts and bruises, borne with the utmost cheerfulness, are the only evil results of an amusement which requires great courage and agility on the part of the competitors for the prizes—that is for the cloths and other things tied to the bullock's horns, and not a little on the part of the mere bystanders. The only time I saw the sport from a place of safety, I was highly delighted with the entertainment and no accident occurred to mar my pleasure. One man was indeed slightly wounded in the buttock, but he was able to walk home and seemed to be as happy as his friends."

Temple, with Street View, Madura.

From a Photo by J. W. H. Joshua, Madura.

CHAPTER V.

OCCUPATIONS, TRADES, ARTS, AND INDUSTRIES.

Madura has at all times been an important centre of commerce and industry. Its central situation in a wide and fertile plain, the demands of an extensive kingdom and the munificent patronage of kings, attracted skilful artisans from far and wide and fostered diverse arts and industries. In recent years its importance as an industrial and commercial centre has very greatly increased and among the causes which have tended to this development we may count the immigration of the Patnulkarans, the opening of the railway line to Pamban and the completion of the Periyar Irrigation Project.

Besides the numerous petty trades and occupations which supply the multifarious wants of a large town population there are a few larger industries for which Madura is famous. Of these especial mention may be made of lacemaking, dyeing, weaving and wood-carving. In former times Madura was famous for its metallic ware also, particularly brass and pewter ware, but these industries are fast dying out. The brass and bellmetal wares on sale in the Pudumantapam are mostly imported articles. The once famous bellmetal kujas, jugs, cups, saucers, tumblers and goglets of Madura are not to be had now. If had at all, the metal is not so pure nor the workmanship so fine. A great deal of this trade has now gone over to Dindigul and Dindigul kujas now enjoy a wide reputation.

Lace-making.—The lace used by the large weaver population is partly imported and partly of local make. French lace is very slowly but surely driving the indigenous lace out of the market. Local silver lace is becoming rare, although local gold lace can still be had on a commercial scale. It is desperately holding its own against the foreigner by virtue of its fineness and durability.

The local process of lacemaking is supposed to be the secret of a few Mussulman families although well worth wide publication. The so-called gold lace is really silver lace finely plated with gold. Silver of the highest purity is chosen and beaten into bars and the bar covered with a thin plate of gold, also of the highest purity. A few indentures are then made on the bar to join the gold to the silver, and the bar is beaten and rounded and passed successively through a graduated series of small holes bored in thick plates of iron. The alloy, if we may call it, is thus drawn out into fine wires. The finest wire has a central silver shaft and an outer golden plate. When the wire has been drawn out to the required fineness it is beaten flat and rolled round a thread of silk. And now you have the finished product.

It is worthy of record that the women, mostly gosha women, largely share the work behind the purdah with the men and show very great skill and dexterity of hand.

The lacemaking industry has given rise to several bye-industries such as the making of jewels of various kinds. Some of the filigree work done by the women is exquisite.

Spinning.—Before speaking of the weaving and dyeing industries it is necessary to say a word about the spinning industry. This is represented by the Madura Mills, Ltd., situated to the north of the railway station. The Company was started by Harvey Brothers in 1892 and the business is in a very flourishing condition. It is proposed to extend the business further and additions to the building are fast progressing. The capital sunk in the business is 10 lakhs of rupees. The mill contains 36,344 spindles and employs 1,600 men, women and children, consumes 2½ million tons of cotton and does spinning, ginning, carding and pressing.

Weaving and Dyeing.—The weaving and dyeing industries are in the hands of the Patnulkarans who occupy the southern half of the town. As one passes along their streets one may see their warps stretched in the street, the men, women and children all busy in their respective duties. Every house is a dyeing and weaving factory and the gutters flow in red colours. Besides these there are large factories in the East Gate streets where one may see extensive grounds for drying yarns and big vats for boiling colours. In recent years some changes have come over the old processes of weaving and dyeing although not to a revolutionary extent. The enlightened few of the community, who have travelled in western countries and studied foreign methods, are trying their very best to introduce improved methods and modern appliances. But their efforts cannot yet be said to have been crowned with success. The conservative instincts of the people, their lack of education and training to handle complicated machinery and the unsuitability to some extent of the modern machines themselves, are obstacles to rapid progress. The old warp and loom still hold their own and primitive processes are still the people's favourites.

Weaving.—Silk and cotton goods of all kinds and grades are woven—saries for women and turbans, with or without lace borders, coloured or uncoloured. All-silk goods are woven only in a few firms. The so called silk weaver is at present more a cotton weaver. The plain white turbans of Madura with lace borders are of a very superior quality and are exported to all parts of the presidency. Coloured turbans find a market in Bombay. Madura lace cloths are valued highly for their rare combination of fine texture and cheapness.

Dyeing.—Madura red cloths were very famous in former days, but they are now going out of the market as a result of the inferior colours produced from the imported aniline and alizarine dyes which have largely replaced the native dyes. But even now the native dyes are preferred to the foreign when durability has to be secured. The Patnuli's dyeing operation is a peculiar process and it is best described in the words of the compiler of the District Gazetteer. He writes :

" *Kamela* powder (collected from the surface glands of the capsules of the tree *Mallotus Plullipinensis*) is used for yellow, lac for red and indigo for blue. The dye called ' Madura red '—is generally made as follows : the ashes of a plant called *umiri* (*salicornia indica*), which grows wild in certain parts of the district, are stirred with cold water and the solution left to stand till the evening. Some of it is then mixed with ground-nut oil (or, if the thread to be dyed is of the finer varieties, with gingelly oil) which becomes emulsified and milky in appearance. In this mordant the thread is soaked all night, and next day it is dried in the sun. This alternate soaking and drying is repeated for ten days and on the eleventh the thread is taken to the Vaigai, (the water of which river is said to be specially favourable to dyeing operations) and left to soak there in running water for some hours. By that time it is beautifully white. Next, the roots of *Oldenlandia umbellata* (chayroot, *imburan* in the vernacular) and the dried leaves of the shrub *Memecylon edule* (Kàyam) are steeped together in water for some time, and to this solution is added some of a German alizarine dye. The thread is again soaked in this for a night, and next boiled for two hours; and then it is taken to the river, left in running water for some time and finally dried in the sun. It is now the fine red colour which is so popular. Deeper shades are obtained by giving additional steepings in the dye solution. For certain special kinds of fabrics the alizarine dye is sometimes replaced by vegetable pigments but this is rare."

Chungudy dyeing.—Equally famous and in great demand are the women's cloths manufactured in Madura and called Chungudies. These are twelve to twenty feet in length—small white rings in a background of red or black. They are either hand-woven or mill-made cloths dyed. It is possible to turn out chungudies by wax printing but the Patnuli would rather have his own old laborious method, and this is how he does it. The portions of the white cloth which represent the white rings in the finished article are first marked off and tied up into little knots and the cloth is then soaked in the dye. The knotted parts are not touched by the colour while all the rest of the cloth is coloured. The Patnuli shows great skill in mixing the colours and varying the designs and, produces cloths of several patterns and varying prices —Rs. 2 to Rs. 50 a piece.

Wood-Carving.—Wood-carving is a speciality in Madura. The temple cars, the vahanams and the Kalyana Mantapam are some of the finest specimens. Some of the best workmen are at present employed by the District Board in their Technical Institute near the Railway Station, and you can find in their show rooms a pretty good collection of various articles of furniture exhibiting some of the finest workmanship. Small rosewood tables supported on fine black wood-elephants are in very great demand with the Anglo-Indian public and are made in large numbers here.

The Technical Institute was established by the District Board in 1890 and continues under their management. Boys of the non-Brahmin castes are given instruction here in carpentry, wood-carving, ivory-carving, metal work, cabinet making and the manufacture of chrome leather articles.

Weaving is not taught in the Technical Institute. The Madura Industrial Association maintains a small factory in which boys of all castes are given a training in weaving. An attempt is made to introduce improved methods in weaving.

The Meenatchi Weaving Factory, situated on the road to the Teppakulam, is built up by native enterprise on the European factory system. It is owned by three go-ahead Patnulis and worked with a capital of three lakhs of rupees. About 300 looms are at work weaving high grade articles in cotton, silk and lace.

Bangle-making.—This is a pretty large industry in Madura, supplying the wants of the native women of all the southern districts of the Presidency. It is in the hands of the Gajula Balijas, a Naik community deriving their name from their occupation. "The process consists in melting lac and brick dust, pounding the result in a mortar, cutting it into strips, moulding these into bangles over a fire and finally decorating them, while still hot, with copper foil, etc.

Copper Wares.—Copper wares are manufactured by a small colony of very industrious Goanese immigrants. They were seen working in a solitary factory some ten years ago, but they have increased tenfold since and you see groups of them busily plying their trade night and day in the street leading from the eastern tower of the temple to the river. They are thrifty folk and seem to have prospered in their trade. They are a self-sufficient lot, scarcely mixing with the natives of the district.

CHAPTER VI.

EDUCATIONAL AND OTHER INSTITUTIONS.

The New Sen Tamil Sangam.—This is a flourishing literary society, established in 1901, for the encouragement of the Tamil language and literature. Among its ardent supporters may be mentioned the Rajahs of Ramnad and Pudukottah, the Zemindar of Palavanatham and many other gentlemen of Madura. Its members number over 500 and include many Tamil scholars and savants of Southern India, Ceylon and foreign universities. It maintains at Madura a boarding institution where facilities are provided for advanced studies in Tamil. A few of the alumni of the institution have already distinguished themselves and have filled the posts of pundits in the Schools and Colleges in and outside Madura. The Library contains over 4,000 books and manuscripts in Tamil, Sanskrit and English. It conducts a high class Tamil Monthly. The Sangam holds annually public examinations of various degrees, and awards certificates of proficiency in Tamil and medals and other honours. Annual conferences for the discussion of matters connected with the Sangam and its objects are held at Madura and other centres. The Sangam is doing useful work by way of original research and by the collection and edition of old and rare Tamil works.

The Union Club.—This institution, started in 1883 and registered in 1907 under Act XXI of 1860, is situated on the northern bank of the Vaigai and to the west of the historic Tamkam Bungalow. Opposite to the Club is the People's Park with its fine walks, fountain and bandstand. The Club has a fine building, an outhouse and grounds.

Mr. C. S. Crole, the then popular Collector of Madura, was chiefly instrumental in bringing the Club into existence and in getting the present site for it, and took considerable interest in its welfare and progress during his tenure of office in Madura. The successive Governors of Madras have been the patrons of the institution. When, in October 1887, Lord Connemara visited it, he was presented with an address of welcome and he expressed himself highly pleased with the objects of the institution.

The present strength of the Club is about 127, consisting mostly of the native gentry of the town. It has a fine Library containing over 1,460 volumes, and a Reading Room. For the recreation of the members lawn tennis and billiards are provided. Under its auspices lectures are occasionally organised and delivered.

The Theosophical Society.—This was started in 1883 under a charter issued to it by Madame H. P. Blavatsky and Col. H. S. Olcott on the application of Mr. (now Sir) S. Subramania Iyer, retired Judge of the High Court of Madras, and several others. Sir S. Subramania Iyer was the President of the Society till he left Madura for Madras as a Member of the Provincial Legislative Council. The Society has been incorporated under Act XXI of 1860. It owns a beautiful and commodious building styled the "Hall of Theosophy." The Library contains over 3,000 volumes and is open to the public. Lectures and religious classes are frequently held under the auspices of the Society. Under the able guidance of the present President the Society has been doing a good deal of useful and charitable work by way of poor relief, religious instruction, female education and on similar lines of public utility. The Sri Minakshi Vidyasala, a Girls School run by the Society, is in a flourishing condition.

The Victoria Edward Library.—At a public meeting held at Madura on 25th October 1902, in connection with the celebration of the Coronation of His late Majesty King Edward VII, it was resolved that a Town Hall with a Library and Museum attached to it, to be styled the Victoria Edward Hall, be erected in the city of Madura as a permanent memorial of the Coronation of His late Majesty as well as in memory of Queen Victoria. At the same meeting an Executive Committee was formed to raise the necessary funds and carry out the objects of the meeting. The Executive Committee succeeded in collecting Rs. 70,800 of which a sum of Rs. 10,500 was spent on the Coronation Day. The balance was invested in Government securities, and out of the proceeds the Library is maintained. It contains about 1,400 volumes and is open to the public. A building is in course of construction to house the Library.

The American Madura Mission.—This Mission owns a Second Grade College and three High Schools besides a few other Secondary and Primary Schools for boys and girls. The College is a fine edifice, put up recently, and is situated on the northern bank of the Vaigai. Hostels for Brahmins and Christians are attached. Extensive grounds for games lie between the main building and the hostels. Originally the College was at Pasumalai, a village two miles to the south-west of Madura. It was started in 1842 as a seminary for the training of native youths for missionary work. Later on classes for secular education were opened. In 1882 the institution was raised to the rank of a Second Grade College with a High School department. A Normal Branch for the training of teachers was opened in 1886. The Hostel was started in 1896. The institution at Pasumalai, which is worth visiting, occupies a large area with extensive grounds for games and quarters for teachers. A small village has sprung up round the school. It has a general library and reading room and a press of its own. The High School department of the College at Madura is located in a building in the west gate.

Belonging to the mission is a Girl's High School with a training section at Mangalapuram on the western outskirts of the town. The American Mission has done a great deal for education in Madura. The Pasumalai College used to be a favourite resort with the students of Southern India.

The Native College.—This was started in 1856 as a Zilla School by the Government and was originally located in the Palace. In 1865 the present buildings were put up, partly with Government aid and partly with public subscriptions, and subsequently the Government handed over the school building and library to a private Committee of Management by whom the institution is now managed. The College department was opened in 1889. New additions made to the building were opened by Lord Wenlock. It is an efficient institution but in recent years, owing to the extension of the railway station, great inconvenience is felt by the bustle and noise. The accommodation is still insufficient and the play-grounds not extensive. Attempts at extensions are in progress. It is rather strange that in spite of the large school-going population, Madura has no College of the first grade. The College has a High School department and many feeder institutions in the town. The Setupathi High School, originally founded by the Rajah of Ramnad, has been amalgamated with the Native College and is managed by the same authorities. It possesses an excellent block of buildings and fine grounds.

The chief newspapers published in the city are the *South Indian Mail*, an English Weekly, and *Vivekabhanu*, a Tamil Journal.

The Mission Hospital.—Opposite to the Palace is situated a beautiful hospital built in the Gothic style belonging to the American Mission. It is a well equipped institution and has accommodation for 48 in-patients. It was erected at a cost of Rs. 42,000, subscribed mostly by the natives of the district. It was opened in 1897 by Sir Arthur Havelock, a former Governor of Madras. It is maintained by annual subscriptions from Nattukottai

Chetties, the Lessees of Sivaganga and others and aids from the Municipality, District Board and the American Mission. It is called the Albert Victor Hospital and is better known after the founder and popular Missionary Surgeon, Dr. Van Allen. Opposite to it is another hospital maintained by the same Mission for women and children, opened in 1898 and doing excellent work.

The Municipal Hospital.—This is located in a beautiful range of buildings in the western part of the town. The Maternity Hospital is located in the historic remains of the guard room of the west gate of the old fort. The Veterinary Hospital is in Tellakulam on the north bank of the river.

The Central Jail.—This stands in the north-east of Madura on the Dindigul road. The building was begun in 1866 with convict labour and finished, at a cost of Rs. 65,000, in 1869. The old district jail was in the building near to the north-east corner of the temple called Mangammal's palace. There are in the jail separate wards for civil debtors and female prisoners.

Mangammal's Choultry—named after the donor, the famous Queen Regent of Madura—is a block of buildings situated just opposite to the Railway Station. Quarters are set apart for Brahmins and other castes, and rooms are available on a small daily rent. They are managed by the District Board. For the maintenance of this and a number of other choultries, lands free of rent had been granted by Mangammal. The property was being mismanaged, so the Government stepped in, resumed the inams, and in their place assigned them tasdik allowances.

CHAPTER VII.

THE HISTORY OF THE JESUIT MISSION IN MADURA.

No account of Madura and its past can be said to be complete without a notice of the activities of the Jesuit Mission that flourished in Madura between 1606 A. D. and 1744 A. D. To the student of local history the subject is of great importance, as the letters and reports sent by the Jesuit Fathers at Madura to their General at Rome from time to time are an invaluable source of information about the history and the social and economic conditions of the Naik Kingdom of Madura during the 17th and 18th centuries. The history of the Society of Jesus forms a brilliant episode in the life of Roman Catholicism, and the Madura Mission was typical of the innumerable Missions the society sent out to various parts of the world. The men that served in Madura were as great as any who belonged to the other Missions of the Society—great in learning and in deeds, as well as in the unflinching devotion to their cause and calm fortitude amidst bitter persecution and great obstacles. The history of this early Mission, its success and its failure, its aims and methods, and its merits and drawbacks, must be full of lessons for the various Christian Missions now working in India. The following brief sketch is based mainly on the English books available on the subject. A fuller account may be found in the letters already referred to and published under the title "La Mission du Madure" by J. Bertrand, S. J., 1844, Paris.

To trace the origin of the Mission we have to go back to the middle of the 16th century, the days of the Counter Reformation and of the beginnings of the Portuguese power in the East. From the latter half of the fifteenth century the Portuguese had sent expeditions to the East and by 1500 had also settled in a few places on the west coast of India. Under the orders of the Portuguese King, some members of the Franciscan Order had accompanied the expeditions to minister to their needs as also to preach the consolations of the divine faith to the heathens of the east. When later, in 1539, the Society of Jesus was formed at Rome under the generalship of St. Ignatius Loyola and Missions were sent out to the different parts of Europe and to the heathen lands beyond the seas, John III King of Portugal, asked the Society to send a Mission to the Portuguese possessions in the East Indies. St. Francis Xavier, an early disciple and associate of St. Ignatius, was selected for the task. Under the patronage and protection of John III, he was put at the head of a small group of Missionaries and sent to India. He reached Goa in 1542 and set to work by starting a seminary there for the training of Missionaries. He himself travelled into the interior of the country and is said to have converted many people to the Christian faith—particularly large numbers of the Paravas of the Fishery Coast, At his instance the Inquisition of Goa was set up for the repression of Judaism and heterodox forms of Christianity. In 1549, after having laboured for seven years in South India, he set sail for Japan, and in 1552, while on a visit to China, he died of fever. His remains were removed and interred in the Church of Bom Jesus at Goa.

Of the batches of Missionaries sent out from the seminary at Goa was the one known as the Madura Mission of Jesuits. The first

Missionary to arrive at Madura was Father Fernandez. He found a few converts there, especially among the Paravas, as a result of the efforts of the Franciscan Friars who were working there. The labours of Father Fernandez between 1592 and 1606 A. D. were not crowned with any great success. He experienced great resistance from all classes. The people looked upon the Portuguese as "parangis" or barbarians who ate the flesh of cows, drank intoxicating liquors and mingled with the lowest classes, the Pariahs not excluded.

In 1606, Madura received another Missionary, a man better able to cope with the situation. This was Robert de Nobili, nephew of Cardinal Bellarmine and a near relation of Pope Marcellus II. When he landed in India, he discovered that the efforts of the Franciscans and St. Francis Xavier had been confined to the conversion of the lower classes of the society and that the higher intellectual classes had not been reached. He attributed the failure of the earlier Missions to this cause and to the employment of methods quite unsuited to the circumstances. He, therefore, set to work from above and began with the proselytisation of the Brahmins. The methods that he employed were also quite novel. With the consent and authority of his superior, the Bishop of Cranganore, he discarded the habit and manners of the European and adopted instead those of the Brahmin. He said to himself: "I will make myself an Indian in order to save the Indians, even as Jesus became a man to save man." Accordingly he donned the yellow robe of the sanyasin, wore the sacred thread on the shoulder and presented himself in Madura as Tatwabodha, a Brahmin from far off western Rome, one of even a higher order than his Indian brother. He eschewed animal food and kept aloof from the Portuguese and other Europeans as well as from the people of the low castes in the country. The task of acquainting himself with the language and literature of the country was an arduous one. But the difficulties of the situation only stimulated the energies of the enthusiast. He secured lodgings in the Brahmin quarters of the town, surrounded himself with a few Brahmin servants and plunged into the study of the sacred literature of the country. In a short time he obtained such a mastery of the Tamil language that visitors were astonished at the purity of his accent and at the fluency of his speech. They were also charmed with his affable and polite manners, and struck with the profundity of his learning and the versatility of his intellect. The foundations of his fame were thus laid and it began to spread. Visitors poured in and common folk thronged at his gate to glean a look of the great rishi. An invitation from the king was declined as being inconsistent with spiritual humility. Having thus overcome the prejudice of the people, he now commenced the holy work of conversion. It was no easy work however. The Brahmin priests were yet doubtful if he was truly a Brahmin. More doubtful were they of the truth of his religion. But he was resolved to satisfy them on both points. He held long disputations with them and those that were convinced—and there were not a few such—embraced the new faith. On one occasion, it is said, he held a long discussion extending over twenty days with a native pundit and succeeded in converting him. More conversions followed in rapid succession. The progress of Christianity was marvellous.

Then came the trouble. The success of the Missionary roused the wrath of the Brahmins. Persecution began. But De Nobili faced it boldly. As Hough, the author of the "History of Christianity in India" says:—"To stop the mouths of his opposers and particularly of those who treated his character of Brahmin as deception, he produced an old, dirty parchment in which he had forged in the ancient Indian characters a deed showing that the Brahmins of Rome were of much older date than those of India, and that the Jesuits of Rome were descended in a direct line from the God Brahma." It is also stated that when the Brahmins expressed a doubt as to the truth of his pretended Brahminhood, he solemnly swore that he was a Brahmin.

The real danger came, however, from quite an unexpected quarter. With the adoption of the Brahminical ways, De Nobili had dissociated himself from Father Fernandez and his low class converts. Moreover, he had permitted his converts to retain their old customs and manners. With him conversion meant nothing more than the substitution of the cross, the images of the Virgin Mary, Peter,

Thomas and the Saints, for the lingam and other Hindu idols. The rites, ceremonies, processions, images, music and other paraphernalia of the Hindu religion were adapted to the needs of the new cult. The success of De Nobili had roused the jealousy of Father Fernandez and the Franciscan friars. His posing as a superior Brahmin and his novel methods excited their hatred. Therefore they made strong representations to the home authorities that he was adopting questionable and unchristian methods, and as a result of these representations he was suddenly suspended from his ministry in 1611 by a peremptory order from Rome. He had not worked for five years before he was thus suspended from his office and he was not permitted to resume his labours for ten years. The progress of Christianity was arrested in the heyday of its success.

The situation that confronted Robert De Nobili now was beset with peculiar difficulties. During the following years, 1611 to 1623, he resided partly at Cochin and partly at Goa and was employed mainly in submitting explanations and disproving the charges levelled against him and in the composition of various works in Tamil and Latin in furtherance of the object that lay next to his heart. Finally he submitted an elaborate reply to the home authorities affirming the harmlessness and expediency of his methods. Indeed so dexterously did he plead his cause that not only was he exonerated, but a special constitution was granted by the Pope reinstating him in office. Nevertheless he was warned against the adoption of idolatrous practices. The attempts of his rivals to thwart his success were thus ultimately foiled. But the interruption of ten years had undone the results of his early endeavours. When he resumed his ministry in 1623, he found himself again face to face with the old obstacles, especially the opposition of the Brahmins. He now left Madura, the scene of his past activities, and toured through Southern India, preaching wherever he went, making converts and establishing congregations wherever conversions took place in large numbers. During the course of the tour he visited Senthamangalam, Salem and Trichinopoly. He worked on amidst great privations, ill-health and persecution. In 1648, in consideration of his failing health and old age, it was thought advisable to post him to Ceylon as Superior of the Mission to that island. The milder climate could do nothing for his rapidly declining health. He was therefore transferred again from there to Mylapore near Madras. Here he built himself a small cottage and spent his last days in the company of his first converts and old associates. His time was now divided between literary composition, prayer and contemplation. After a very brief span of rest here, he died in 1656. He was beyond doubt the greatest of the Missionaries sent out to India by the Society of Jesus. He was the real founder of the Madura Mission. He brought his genius to bear upon missionary problems. His methods were quite original and were attended with phenomenal success. Accurate knowledge of the religion, the literature and the people of the country, complete mastery of the vernaculars with a view to fluency of speech and writing, adoption of harmless native customs and ceremonies, were some of the means that he employed with great success. Though the propriety of his methods has been questioned, it can never be said that he ever lost sight of the real object of his mission.

Among the literary productions of the great Missionary may be mentioned the Gnanopadesa—an elaborate disquisition on the attributes of the deity expressed in felicitous Tamil; the Mantramalai containing the principal part of the Roman liturgy and composed in a highly classical style; and the fifth Veda—a very curious work composed with materials taken from the Bible. "It is interesting to note," writes the author of the 'History of Christianity in India,' "that this fifth Veda after many adventures reached the hands of Voltaire who presented it in 1761 to the library of the King of France as a literary curiosity."

After the retirement of Robert De Nobili from Madura, the work of the Mission was carried on by other members of the Jesuit Order. Fathers Vico, Martinz, DaCosta, and Alvarez were in charge in turn. In their time the field of activity was extended over the modern districts of Tanjore, Trichinopoly, Salem and Coimbatore. In spite of persecution the number of converts increased and churches were built in various parts of the country. Converts were made from all castes, though the Pariahs and Kallans and Maravars, the lower classes of Hindus, formed the rank and file of the neophytes. The system of caste was not swept away, but perpetuated among the converts. The native clergymen were accordingly divided into two classes for the more effective dissemination of the faith—the Brahmin sanyasins who ministered to the Brahmin converts, and the Pandaram Missionaries who looked after the non-Brahmin converts.

The Jesuit Fathers who were at the head of the Brahmin sanyasins adopted Brahminical customs and manners, styled themselves gurus, gave themselves native names and wore yellow robes in the fashion of the sanyasins. They made frequent ablutions, marked their forehead with sandal paste and abstained from animal food and intoxicating liquors. In short, they moved about among the converts to the new faith exactly like, and passed for, Brahmins, living solely on vegetables and milk and dissociating themselves from the lower castes.

About the year 1693 a wave of persecution swept over the Marava country of Ramnad, and the Christians suffered great hardships. The cause of the outburst seems to have been the conversion of a Sethupathi Prince by John de Britto. De Britto had succeeded Alvarez as the head of the Pandaram Missionaries, and pushed his activities into the Marava country. The story goes that on one occasion he cured a Prince of the Sethupathi Dynasty of an incurable disease and the latter immediately renounced his national faith, abandoned his harem and followed the lead of De Britto. This caused a tumult in the household, and when the news reached the ears of the Sethupathi, he sent an order for the arrest of the Jesuit Father. De Britto was surprised in his cottage and taken captive to Ramnad. He was subjected to great cruelties on the way, but he bore them patiently. After a long period of confinement in Ramnad, he was summoned before a tribunal and sentenced to be banished from the kingdom. But he was not allowed to escape with his life. He was overtaken on his way, not far from Ramnad, and beheaded under the secret orders of the Sethupathi, and his mutilated body was exposed publicly as a warning to others. Such was the end of another of the great Missionaries that Christendom sent to the East. The scene of his martyrdom became a place of pilgrimage to the later generations of Christians, and miracles are said to have been wrought there.

A few words about the early life of this martyr may not be out of place. Jean Hector de Britto was born in Lisbon, in 1647, of a distinguished Portuguese noble family. As a boy he was chosen to be the playmate of the Crown Prince of Portugal, and was brought up under the special care of King Pedro IV. His education was put into the hands of the Jesuits. Early in life he felt a call to enter their ranks. His affectionate mother and the royal patron prevented him from joining the Order until, in 1662, he was free to act and took orders. Ten years later he was sent out to India and was appointed Superior of the Madura Mission. He acquitted himself so well in this capacity that in 1688 he was appointed Procurer and as such had to go back to his native country. On his arrival there he was received with great honour by all, the King as well as the people. The universities conferred honours upon him. After some time, the Bishopric of Cranganore in India was offered to him. But he declined the high post and chose in 1691 to serve as a simple missionary in the Marava country where, we saw, he met with his martyrdom. The persecution that overtook him raged for five years longer.

Of the later missionaries who distinguished themselves, the most conspicuous was Father Beschi. He was also the most distinguished among the Jesuits for learning and intellect. He made Trichinopoly the chief centre of his activities and is said to have enjoyed great influence with the rulers of the country. His knowledge of Tamil was deep and he wielded a facile pen. His best known composition was a Tamil work of great literary merit. It treated of scriptural subjects and contained, like the Hindu Puranas, high ethical teaching. Another was a prose work in Tamil on didactic and doctrinal subjects. He also wrote a commentary on the Kural in Tamil. His largest work was a Tamil Latin dictionary composed about 1726.

In 1759, the Society of Jesus was suppressed in Portugal for political reasons and the movement against it spread rapidly to France and other countries of Europe. In 1773, owing to external pressure, Pope Clement XIV formally issued a Bull abolishing the Order altogether. It was not long before the effects of the suppression of the Society in Europe were felt in India. "In 1759, when the Order of the Jesuits was suppressed in Portugal, a vessel came to Goa with orders from the King, and all the fathers, 127 in number, were put in prison and distributed among the monasteries of Goa. Then they were all crowded together in a jail where the windows were walled up and the door shut except when the police were present. On the 2nd December 1759, all were embarked for Portugal on a vessel fitted to receive not more than forty or fifty. There they were treated as prisoners of war, receiving but one meal a day. Twenty-six other passengers were loaded with irons for showing compassion to the unfortunate priests. Twenty-four priests died of scurvy. The rest struggled with death five months and debarked at Lisbon May 24, 1760. Some were taken to the prisons of Taferies, one was sent to the castle of St. Julien. One group of ten Italians, three Germans, two Spaniards, one Frenchman and one of some other nationality were cast into dungeons, than which the subterranean galleries of the catacombs could hardly be worse. Air holes in the ceiling were scarce; there were two doors, but they opened only to the police"*.

The Madura Mission came to an end along with the general suppression of the Jesuits. The native Christians were left to shift for themselves and disappeared in a short time. Thus ended one of the most brilliant chapters in the history of the Christian Missions to the East.